Presented to

From

Date

Endorsements

In my most recent book published by Charisma House, *The Passover Prophecies: How God is Realigning Hearts and Nations in Crisis*, I wrote, "We must be a people of imagination like the early pioneers of nations. Isaiah 26 is wonderfully translated in the Passion Translation Bible. I love the way verse 3 is phrased: *those whose imaginations are consumed with you* (Isa. 26:3). The Hebrew word translated "imagination" is *yester*, meaning "form, concept, framework, imagination, mind". A human imagination wholly owned by the Holy Spirit is one of the most powerful redemptive forces on earth.

These times call for a critical, God-filled imagination. This will create a new framework and conceptualization of all the problems around us. Our minds should be fixed on and become consumed by Him. This is what will unleash the supernatural creativity resident in all of the redeemed and will give birth to the exploits necessary for our triumph. In this season, we must reform our minds and imaginations. We must gather raw materials, then shape them into form and identify our future. Our concepts, frameworks, minds and imaginations must unlock into new forms and identities to meet and triumph in the era ahead.

Dr. Barbie Breathitt's five book series, *IMAGINE*, has captured the essence of God's plans to reinvent the church in the fullness of Christ's creative, life-giving, resurrection power with signs and wonders following. Each individual believer must take on his or her Christlike identity as a Son of God to move forward into this era, as One New Man arises to demonstrate God's glory on earth as it is in heaven!

Dr. Chuck D. Pierce
President, Glory of Zion International Ministries
President, Global Spheres in Corinth, Texas

God's ways are higher than our ways, and yet we are invited to co-labor with Christ as partakers in His divine nature. Pioneering ideas in her new book series *IMAGINE*, will open you up to your limitless potential. You will come to know that God created you to navigate life with the mind of Christ, and by faith, you can tap into a Spirit-inspired, creative process that is aligned with God's heart.

Dr. Breathitt's books will help you to understand your call to walk in a prophetic relationship with Jesus and to unlock the powerful truths available to all who believe in Him. This is a fresh invitation to imagine with God, to dream with Him for the future and to access and implement heaven's answers to the world's problems to advance God's Kingdom.

Dr. Ché Ahn
Founder and President, Harvest International Ministry
Founding and Senior Pastor, HROCK Church, Pasadena, CA
International Chancellor, Wagner University
Founder, Ché Ahn Ministries

Many copy or imitate others. Some create a model for others to learn from, and some are innovative. But few are innovators. Others learn a subject matter, then reach a peak and just plain plateau and cease advancing. Then there are those who become constant learners as a lifestyle, filling their heart and soul with the creative realms of God. Dr. Barbie Breathitt is cut from this type of creative fabric.

As an educator and prophetic interpreter/analyst, this consecrated woman of God consistently takes us on an exciting journey of discovery. Can you imagine that? As you partake of Barbie's teachings and her adventurous spirit carved from the boundaries of the Word of God, you, too, will grow in your prophetic imagination into a place where dreams really do come true!

Dr. James W Goll
Founder, God Encounters Ministries and GOLL Ideation LLC
Life Language Communications Coach

Dr. Barbie L. Breathitt is on the cutting edge of using her God-appointed seer gifting to help people gain an enhanced understanding of how God created and operates through the imagination, so that His people can apprehend the mysteries and purposes of God and manifest His glory in the earthly realm."

Cindy Jacobs
Generals International, Dallas, Texas

Beautiful, wonderful and full of divine insight! *IMAGINE* provides the 'missing link' in Christian understanding and practice between the natural and the supernatural realms that many believers have been seeking for years. Dr. Barbie Breathitt has done the body of Christ a great service by providing a solid biblical foundation for understanding how the natural and spiritual interact—how we integrate that process into our own lives by cooperating with the Holy Spirit.

These books are both paradigm-changing and life-altering. It is a wonderful blend of contemplative and analytical biblical thinking, personal experience building and divine revelation that will provide earnest believers with a new blueprint for the kind of walk with God they have always yearned for.

I suggest you read these books slowly and thoughtfully, perhaps several times, because it redefines the normative Christian experience in many fundamental ways. As you train your senses (Hebrews 5:14) this way, you will find yourself thinking all things have become new for me now.

Joan Hunter
Author/Healing Evangelist
Host, TV Show *Miracles Happen*

Dr. Barbie Breathitt's book series *IMAGINE* is a timely message, as this is the hour that God is releasing creative thinking and solutions from heaven. These books will open doorways to anointed thinking and the ability to see in the Spirit. This will activate your ability to dream and create at new levels through the Holy Spirit. This series is grounded in sound biblical teaching and practical instructions of how to apply it to your daily life. It is not just for creative dreamers, seers or songwriters—it is applicable to all the gifts, especially in business and ministry.

Doug Addison
Doug Addison.com
Author, webcast *Hearing God Everyday*, podcast *Daily Prophetic Words*, and prophetic blog *Spirit Connection*

Perfect, absolute peace surrounds those whose imaginations are consumed with you (Isaiah 26:3 TPT). Our imagination enables us to envision the Invisible One and thereby, as Barbie wrote, '…to redesign the image of ourselves.' The imagination is uncharted territory for Christians. We need more people like Dr. Breathitt to lead the way.

Ron Campbell

In her *IMAGINE* series, Dr. Barbie Breathitt's intensity of personae invites readers to partake in her deep insights, advanced levels of understanding and supernatural operations of faith in the glory realm. She challenges us not only to dream but also dares us to courageously imagine the impossible. Barbie creatively inspires us to unlock our potential in Christ through our imagination, to transcend the limitations of the flesh and progress in the limitless dimensions of God's glory.

I was often labeled as and teased about being a fantasizer during my childhood years, which greatly stifled the use of my imagination. The *IMAGINE* series has now unlocked the door to my imaginativeness, allowing me to freely and confidently advance. I have been awakened to the vast dimensions of God consciousness and His power, which equip me to exist and operate far beyond my God-given anointings and giftings. This series empowers me to live my future in the now!

Michael Adeyemi Adefarasin
Kingdom Lifeline Apostolic Ministries (KLAM), Abuja, Nigeria

A new era has dawned for God's people! A newfound season of supernatural revelation is being released from heaven to those who have the spiritual eyes and ears to see and hear what the Spirit is doing and saying (see Revelation 3:22).

Dr. Barbie Breathitt's *IMAGINE* series issues a clarion call for Believers to arise and supplant the old nature and attain their new identity in Christ. She implores readers to take on the very nature of Christ. She encourages them to utilize their divine imagination to create and decree their God-purposed destinies into reality in the same way God imagined and created before the beginning of time. Readers will discover the fundamental knowledge of how to apply their infinite imagination to shape their individual lives, influence the world and execute God's purposes.

Allow Barbie's *IMAGINE* series to transform your mind and usher you into a higher dimension of the Lord's destiny for your life!

Barbara Wentroble
President, International Breakthrough Ministries (IbM)
President, Breakthrough Business Leaders (BBL)
Author, Releasing the Voice of the Ekklesia; Becoming a Wealth Creator; Council Room of the Lord (series)

Works by the Author

Angels in God's Kingdom

Dream Encounters: Seeing Your Destiny from God's Perspective

Gateway to the Seer Realm: Look Again to See Beyond the Natural

So You Want to Change the World?

Hearing and Understanding the Voice of God

Dream Seer: Searching for the Face of the Invisible

Dream Interpreter

A to Z Dream Symbology Dictionary

Volume I Dream Symbols

Volume II Dream Symbols

Volume III Dream Symbols

Action Dream Symbols

When Will My Dreams Come True?

Dream Sexology

Sports & Recreation Dream Symbols

IMAGINE

TRANSFORMING INTO YOUR NEW IDENTITY

Dr. Barbie Breathitt

VOLUME 2

Breath of the Spirit Ministries, Inc.
P.O. Box 1356
Lake Dallas, Texas 75065
BarbieBreathitt.com
BarbieBreathittEnterprises.com
DreamsDecoder.com

ISBN-13: 978-1-942551-06-5

Published by: Barbie Breathitt Enterprises, Inc.

Printed in Canada.

Dedication

It is my deepest honor to dedicate my series of five *IMAGINE* books to my best friend, personal confidant and beautiful baby sister, Brenda Doreen Breathitt. She was born in Lakeland, Florida on October 29, 1966 and transitioned into Heaven on Saturday, September 7, 2019 at the age of fifty-two. Brenda was a brilliant light of joy with an excellent sense of humor that caused us all to laugh. Her warm, inviting smile disarmed people, letting them know she was a safe place to share their hearts. Brenda was clothed with grace, compassion and beauty that sprang up from a deep well within her loving heart. Her caring concern for others exuded from her countenance to bless all those who knew her. Brenda was full of godly strength and dignity.

Brenda's name meant *the glory of God's sword. Let all who seek You rejoice and be glad in You; and let those who love Your salvation say continually, let God be magnified* (Psalm 70:4). She laughed and loved well through her painful battle with cancer knowing in the days to come she had a home in heaven. Her thoughts and prayers were with her unsaved friends and family members that she was leaving behind. She spoke with wisdom and godly counsel always carrying faithful instruction on her tongue. She diligently watched over her family, friends and household never eating the bread of idleness. Her only daughter Chelsea arises to call her blessed. There are many women who do noble things, but Brenda's loving nature, quick wit, sterling character and integrity surpassed them all. We all know that charm is deceptive, and physical beauty is fleeting; but I praise Brenda for she was a woman who feared the Lord. Those who had the chance to know Brenda honor her memory for all that her hands have done. No matter where Brenda went she always found a friend. Her sweet words of comfort bring her praise from the city gates. Brenda blessed so many in her life with unconditional love, a listening ear, and words of encouragement, profound humor and a shared smile. Brenda made all of us better people for having known her. She is sorely missed.

Barbie

Thank You

A special thank you to heaven's Prophetic Poet Keat Wade for sharing the amazing poems he has authored in his four amazing books: *For Whom Beyond Beckons, Dueling Kingdoms: Chronicling the Times, A Gnarled Tree and Me,* and *Chronology of Love: Times and Seasons.* All of his incredible poems are available on Amazon.com and through Christian Publishing Xulon Press.

Keat Wade's poems are unique in three ways, (1) the supernatural way poems are received (2) the visual of what is going on in the supernatural realm (3) and being in sync with God's Timing (Hebrew Calendar). Keat Wade shares intimate conversations with the Almighty. He only writes what he hears. Keat hears or visually sees either the title or the first line. Nothing more comes until he starts to write. Then the words flow in poem form as a divine download, complete in one setting. Keat feels drawn into that supernatural realm until the words are complete. Then it lifts. The poems reflecting the Timing of God picture what God is doing in the supernatural realm, thus giving confirmation or direction.

Keat is a graduate of Fort Hays State University. He is a writer by desire and academically prepared with a Bachelor of Arts degree in English and Speech and a Master of Education degree in guidance and counseling. Keat retired from his teaching at Oklahoma Wesleyan University. Keat and Judy Garlow Wade now live in the San Diego area where his prophetic writing began.

Foreword

God is restoring our vision with provision.

Dr. Barbie Breathitt's *IMAGINE* series persuasively inspires Believers to embark on a journey of self-discovery, seeking and finding God and to discover His hidden, concealed mysteries through their sanctified imagination.

Readers will be immersed in God's truth and transformed by fresh revelation, soundly based on Scripture, crucial to this new season of operating in supernatural strength, powerful influence and Christ's authority. One is introduced to the aspects and mighty functions of the Holy Spirit, the Seven Spirits of God, God's communication conduits (dreams and visions) and how to use the awakened imagination to pray effectively, tap into unlimited favor and blessings, access healing and manifest miracles.

This is a new day of opportunity. Our divine imagination affords us the ability to know and receive all that God has destined for us to be and accomplish. It is time to increase and expand our borders. Barbie's writings challenge us to disconnect from the religious, legalistic ways of reasoning and exchange them for the creative, life-giving mind of Christ.

These volumes stir us to imagine the impossible, to consider how we think, what we believe and how we relate to God Almighty and others so that we can become Christlike, accurately discern God's plans and purposes and manifest His glory for His Kingdom advancement. Barbie has managed to successfully use applicable Scripture-based examples and captivating stories throughout the series to enlighten, encourage and guide us through a spiritual conversion of our identity that empowers us to apprehend our extraordinary future.

Our God-designed, ingenious imagination births visions of the unknown things of God and brings the invisible realms of creation into focus so it can become a reality in our lives. What we create and see in our imagination causes us to encounter and experience a broader dimension of God.

God's Spirit is advancing and positioning us through the use of our divine imagination to equip us with wisdom, revelation, fresh anointings and unlimited prosperity in order to draw the lost, sick and dying unto Christ.

Dr. John P. Kelly
Convener, International Coalition of Apostolic Leaders
InternationalCoalitionofApostolicLeaders.com

Contents

Introduction

God desires His beloveds to know Him intimately, to witness, experience and fully function in His glory by operating in a higher, more advanced state of being and manifesting the Seven Spirits of God. We learned in the first volume this is only possible by being Christ-conscious and using our amazing, God-given imagination. By understanding what it is and how to enter into rest, we are able to comprehend spiritual truth, wisdom and revelation knowledge accessed by faith that is available to us through the use of our amazingly God-designed platform—our awakened imagination. The imagination is the key to the infinite doors of opportunity that lead into the boundless expanses of God.

Our spirit has the highest calling and function; it is finer tuned than the natural, carnal soul. The spirit and soul battle for the ultimate control. *It is He who, coming after me, is preferred before me* (John1:17). We must transition from the carnal mindset to a divine mindset by adopting the mind of Christ in order to advance the Kingdom of God. We must take on a new, Christlike identity to operate with the faith of God, to declare, prophesy and move as the Almighty directs so that we may fulfill His plans and purposes for us individually and as the Body of Christ.

The first man, Adam (means *formed of the earth in God's image*), fell to the sinful desires of the soul. Christ is the second Adam, who came as a perfect man to redeem the souls of mankind. *The first man was of the earth, made of dust; the second Man is the Lord from heaven* (1 Corinthians 15:47). Born-again Believers have a spiritual body in heaven just like the Lord Jesus Christ. At the moment of our physical conception, a microscopic fraction of God's light comes into the cell's structure. The instant the male sperm penetrates the cell wall to unite with the female ovum, a new life is created as a beautiful (living) human soul.

When we are born again, the divine light of God permeates every cell of our being. The presence of God creates an aura of spiritual light that causes us to:

> *Arise, and shine; for our light has come! And the glory of the LORD is raised upon us. For behold, the darkness shall cover the earth, and deep darkness the people; but the Lord will arise over us, and His glory will be seen upon us. The Gentiles shall come to our light, and kings to the brightness of our rising* (Isaiah 60:1–3).

God's creative light is assimilated throughout our entire body to form our unique DNA, special gifts, talents, personality and specific features.

The radiant light of God dwelling within us ignites the anointing and spiritual favors that empower the manifestation of the glory realms. Our eternal soul and spirit are formed and held together by God's presence. We live, move and have our being through the creative holding power of this minuscule God-particle of light, also known by science as *The Higgs Boson.*

At the moment of our salvation, the light of God comes in at a greater, increased measure than that of the light of God released at our conception. The saving light of God removes darkness from our being. The magnificent light of God's love and all of God's glorious IAM names, characteristics and attributes are imparted into our being. The powerful forces of God's names are infused into the spirit of every Believer. The attributes of God are hidden deep within us. These traits reside in a place of rest waiting for us to discover their existence.

> *The imagination is the key to the infinite doors of opportunity that lead into the boundless expanses of God.*

When we learn of their existence, we then must discover how to access and operate in them through the power of love. When Believers grow in their hunger and thirst for righteousness, we mature in our spiritual understanding. Divine intelligence comes to us through the knowledge of Christ that activates the power found in the different names, characteristics and various attributes of God's power and authority within us.

As we mature and grow in the ministry of prayer (continually practicing the presence of God), the authority that the Holy Spirit grants us brings an increased measure of knowledge. We learn to understand the innumerable, different ways in which the Spirit of God moves. Through faith, we tap into the attributes and then clothe ourselves in the characteristics of God's powerful names. His glorious light, anointings and the endless, beautiful frequencies of the Divine reveal Him as our unlimited source of power. Once we know how to accurately identify and operate our spiritual gifts at a mature level in the realms of anointing and faith, God faithfully promotes us into the unlimited realms of glory.

Moses was shown God's goodness, and his face shone as a reflection of the light of God's glory.

> *Then God said, "I will make ALL My goodness to pass before you, and I will proclaim the names of the Lord before you. I will be gracious to whom I will be gracious, and I will have compassion on whom I will have compassion"* (Exodus 33:19).

When we are saved from sin, baptized in water and then baptized again in the Holy Spirit and fire, God's unlimited power and light are multiplied within us.

Overcoming the struggles of life strengthen, stretch and enlarge our capacity to love and hold more of God's presence. Difficulties empower us to take the present challenge to break out of the restrictive cocoon of our old identity. Whether our previous identity was good, bad or ugly, God has planned more for us. God has something far greater in store for each of us. *They shall see His face, and His name shall be on their foreheads* (Revelation 22:4).

My prophetic friend Clancy had a dream of me emerging out of a cocoon with a set of large, beautiful, rainbow-colored wings. She said, "Barbie, at first you struggled in this new Isaiah 11:2, Revelation 4:5 season. You were not comfortable in the process of learning how to operate in this new level of power to manifest the Seven Spirits of God."

It is the process of struggling to emerge into a higher state of being that makes us strong. If we never learn to stand on our own two feet, we will be open to being controlled or dominated. We will remain a codependent, weak, victim-minded person who always relies on others for everything. But if we will take on our new, Christlike identity, we will emerge and move as an innovative creation who is full of the confidence of Christ.

We must transition from the carnal mindset to the mind of Christ in order to advance the Kingdom of God.

Each one of the names of God empowers us to open the door of access to a different realm of anointing. Doors represent a conscious awareness of a new opportunity or dimension that is available. Our promotion is accelerated when we come into the revelation knowledge and understanding of how the power contained in that one of His names works. These various realms empower us to operate in miracles, signs and wonders, to invent, create and gather wealth, to prosper in the power and to obtain astute, spiritual perception, revelation knowledge and authority of the unlimited realms of glory.

Each of the names of God grant the awakened imagination the keys of wisdom that are needed to access the divine light found in God's revelation knowledge. Heaven relates to us according to the amount of enlightenment we have sought and spiritual understanding we have gained and operate in.

When the imagination is at work, the brain is illuminated with light. The imagination causes the pillar of fire to burn brightly, arise and move within the mind of the Believer. We understand the ways and things of the Spirit through the revelation knowledge that we possess about Christ.

God has over 365 different names. Each one of God's names that indwells us also has corresponding attributes, characteristics and power to ignite and infuse our spirit by highlighting our God-given gifts. We are called to take on and utilize the power found in the names of God to change our individual lives and to shift nations.

The Holy Spirit empowers us to achieve our grand destiny as we trust in and rely on the illuminating power of Christ's love. *Before I formed you in the womb, I knew you, and before you were born, I consecrated you; I have appointed you a prophet to the nations* (Jeremiah 1:5).

When the spirit of man is born again, the presence of God's light force emerges from within. Then the light of revelation continues to expand beyond the body. The outshining of God's light breaks us out of any predisposed parameters by moving us past the limitations of the soul's boundaries.

The rebirth of the human spirit ignites the ever-expanding power of God that continues to grow within us until it reaches out and above the natural realm to exceed the soul's desires. In the marketplace, outside the four walls of the church, the shadow of Peter (the outshining of the glory cloud), which expanded past his body, touched, healed and delivered those with whom his spirit came in contact.

When we are born again from heaven above of both Spirit and water, we become heirs of God. We tap into the mind of Christ and become partakers of His divine nature. *Seek the Lord and His strength; seek His face evermore* (1 Chronicles 16:11)!

> God's creative light is assimilated throughout our entire body to form our unique DNA, special gifts, talents, personality and specific features.

The Spirit of God resting in the consciousness of the Believer's spirit teaches him or her how to rule the body by submitting the will of the soul to the spirit.

> *But the natural man does not receive the things of the Spirit of God, for they are foolishness to him; nor can he know them, because they are spiritually discerned. But he who is spiritual, judges All Things, yet he himself is rightly judged by no one. For who has known the mind of the Lord that he may instruct Him? But we have the mind of Christ* (1 Corinthians 2:14–16).

Until we activate our imagination through seeing ourself becoming the attribute, that characteristic with the capacity to house that level of power that is resident in that particular name of God, we are not able to access the transformational authority and receive that ability, aptitude or potential in our waking life.

CHAPTER ONE

The Spirit of the Word

God is the brilliant Father of Light. His living Word is a master key that is a powerful, creative light force. God sends His Word to heal and deliver us from all forms of destruction. His Word will never return to Him void; instead, it will undertake and complete what it was sent to accomplish. The light beam of God's Word illumines our path, causing us to see where to step in the dark (see Psalm 119:105).

The positive, living words we speak and the creative words spoken over us have the power to generate life. Inspirational words that are believed have the capacity to shift us into a higher sphere of increase. Motivational words have the ability to multiply our influence. Constructive words stimulate our thoughts and encourage us to prosper by always changing things for the better.

The measure of active godlike faith we incorporate in our waking life will determine the spiritual and physical fortunes we will acquire in this life and into eternity.

> *In the beginning, I* (wisdom) *was there, for God possessed me even before He created the universe. From eternity past I was set in place, before the world began. I was anointed from the beginning* (Proverbs 8:22–23).

God's promise to us is that He will restore deliverers and wise counselors to the world as they were in former times, so we can be at peace, living in righteous, faith-filled mansions.

It is God who has called each of us by name, even before we were born He knew all about us. It is the Spirit of God that leads us forward on a prosperous, successful path. As we listen to and draw near to God, we learn to walk together as one with and in Him. God does not speak in secret riddles to His intimate friends and beloved Bride. He is always a present help in the times of our every need. He empowers us step-by-step, teaching us to succeed by His Spirit. Our part is to listen and be obedient to His commands, so that His joy, peace and love will spring up and flow through us like a mighty river. The rippling levels of success are drawn to us, just like the continuous waves of the sea wash over and deposit treasures on the shoreline.

> *The positive words we speak and the creative words spoken over us have the power to generate life.*

In the very beginning, the living expression of God's Word was already resting there with God Almighty Himself. The two of them were together, intermingled, dwelling face-to-face in intimacy. When Jesus walked the earth as the Living Word, He knew from the beginning who would be His skeptics, critics and traitors. He did not disclose this to His disciples, because He was still with them. But just as Jesus spoke to John on the Isle of Patmos, His voice is breaking the silence and beckoning us to ascend into a higher mansion, so He can reveal to us what must happen after this (see Revelation 4:1).

When we become aware of Christ calling us upward to hear His heart's cry, we will conceive from His creative DNA and transcend our conception of ourselves, believing that we have become that which He has designed us to be.

In the Era of the Mouth, we must learn to be speaking spirits who decree the Word of God in the increased measure of the faith of God. The measure of faith we possess will ensure that the Word of God going forth from our mouth is fulfilled and does not return to us void. God's Word is designed with the power that is necessary to cause us to prosper and fulfill His purposes here on earth (see Isaiah 55:11). As Believers, we must not mask or muzzle the words of our mouths, to dampen or stamp out our message of hope and love to a dark, desperate world.

The circumstances, people and things that exist in our life today are there because of our own beliefs, designing words and decrees. Our spoken words have created them. Words have the power to create spiritual enlightenment, love, peace and joy, or they have the power to release the hate-filled, murderous destruction of darkness. The words we speak form an alliance with the death and destruction of the kingdom of darkness or with the overcoming kingdom of light, love and eternal life.

God is able to make All Things work together for our good when we are submitted to His will. The light of God's Word forgives, cleanses and removes the darkness of our past. His light heals what is sick, renovates the diseased and reestablishes the broken with a fortification of strength. The Word of God delivers us from what has bound us and restores to us what was surrendered, lost or stolen. The Word of God is nearer to you than your breath; it permeates every cell of your being. The Word is resident in your heart, even living within your very mouth.

We have been given the power to choose Jesus, the Living Word of Life. His divine blessings bring spiritual healing, increased life and the multiplication of riches. The degree to which we intimately engage Jesus, in order to discover and know His ways, will determine the height, breadth and depth in which our personal well-being will flow, as well as our corporate prosperity. If we allow spiritual blindness to bring forth a gloomy fear of failure, the opportunity at hand will be lost. If we choose to be complacent, idle or depressed, instead of pursuing God with all of our heart, we have, in a sense, already given up. The dream will die. Consequently, the finality of a dream's death will overtake us, and the hope of our vision being fulfilled will slip from our hands and fade away.

God's Word is designed with the power that is necessary to cause us to prosper and fulfill His purposes here on earth.

A negative misinterpretation of a dream or any situation or relationship in life that is full of skepticism, uncertainty or reservation can execute a death sentence to that dream, situation or relationship. Fear, doubt and unbelief can cause us to execute things at the wrong time, which can have devastating consequences. We either make mistakes by prematurely taking action or by delaying action, due to hesitation, confusion or distrust.

> *Not that I have already attained, or am already perfected; but I press on, that I may lay hold of that for which Christ Jesus has also laid hold of me. Brethren, I do not count myself to have apprehended; but one thing I do, forgetting those things which are behind* (the painful traumas, past mistakes) *and reaching forward to those things which are ahead,* (confidently imagining a bright, beautiful and prosperous future) *I press toward the goal for the prize of the upward call of God in Christ Jesus. Therefore, let us, as many as are mature, have this* (Christlike, imaginative) *mind and if in anything you think otherwise, God will reveal even this to you. Nevertheless, to the degree that we have already attained, let us walk by the same rule, let us be of the same* (Christlike, imaginative) *mind* (Philippians 3:12–16).

The imaginative mind of God is the creative light force that fills the void places of our lives. God's Word causes a spiritual fatness that breaks off restrictive yokes or anything else that tries to bind, limit, blind or deceive us. God's glorious light dispels all darkness. The Three in One manifests in legions of multifaceted dimensions of wisdom and endless spiritual levels, all in the consciousness of one divine, loving and eternal being.

God is a devoted creator! He is the imaginative source of all that exists in the universe. The three-in-one God Almighty rises from within us, overshadows and comes to visit us in various and diverse ways. The Holy Spirit fills us to the utmost capacity, consuming every fiber of our being. Christ empties, broadens and reforms us so that we can contain more of His glory. As a result, the River of God flows out of us with the strength of His overcoming wisdom and His creative, life-giving and miracle-working power.

When we prophesy as God commands, the faith residing deep within fills us, rises to the surface, surrounds, covers and rests upon us. The Holy Spirit's animated force floods, moves and reconnects the scattered dry bones that have fallen in barren, desert places. *I tell you that He will avenge them speedily. Nevertheless, when the Son of Man comes, will He really find faith on the earth* (Luke 18:8)?

When God comes to visit in a new way, He is drawn to our expectant faith. His desire is for us to know Him in that fresh dimension or active way of movement. Jesus' beautiful face makes room for the brilliance of His countenance to shine into the depths of our being.

> *In the beginning God created the heavens and the earth* (out of His grand imagination). *The earth was without form, and void; and darkness was on the face of the deep. And the* (creative, energetic, life-giving) *Spirit of God was hovering over the face of the waters. Then God said, "Let there be light," and there was light. And God saw the light that it was good; and God divided the light from the darkness* (Genesis 1:1–4).

Daily, Christ reveals fresh elements of the length of His nature, the features of the heights of His characteristics and the widths of the facets of His attributes. The radiant breadth of the Father of Light's presence shines forth to touch, transform and enlighten every one of us so that we may rediscover our Creator and find our God. He is the creator, author and finisher of our destiny.

God's divine light shows us the gifts and talents that have always been present and hidden deep within us. These skills and abilities are now being uncovered and revealed to us by the illuminating light of God's glorious countenance. *For it is the God who commanded light to shine out of darkness, who has shone in our hearts to give the light of the knowledge of the glory of God in the face of Jesus Christ* (2 Corinthians 4:6).

> *When we prophesy as God commands, the faith residing deep within us rises to the surface, surrounds and rests upon us.*

When the Christ within reveals His glorious light of revelation, the Believer gains spiritual sight, knowledge and wisdom, and he or she sheds the scales of blind ignorance. *The Holy Spirit reveals deep and hidden things; He knows what lies in darkness, and light dwells with Him* (Daniel 2:22).

With the clarity of newfound spiritual vision (refer to Realms of Vision in Volume I), our eyes are opened to see God's revelation knowledge. Our imagination must observe future events in a much larger multidimensional, invisible world before they can manifest and occur within us and on earth. In that place of vision, we hear the spoken Word, and we see the power of it demonstrated before us.

Hearing the spoken Word of God gives us the measure of belief needed to discern and understand the Holy Spirit's clear strategy to attract, capture and pull success into our present. In other words, faith causes a plan to be created, which enables us to move the abundance of the future into our now. Our focused, faith-filled prayers, decrees and declarations give our imagination's visions entrance into the physical world.

Writing the vision out empowers us to define exactly what we want and to see it clearly. By writing the vision down, we hold the four-dimensional door of the imagination open. With the four-dimensional door open, we can bring out to display (in the solid, tangible three-dimensional world of our current reality) what was believed, seen and heard by us while we visited in the past, present and future mansions in the realm of the Spirit. Writing the revelation down empowers us to develop a working plan and strategy to cause what we have only imagined to manifest (to be established) in the natural realm.

Hearing the spoken Word gives us the measure of belief needed to discern and understand the Holy Spirit's clear strategy to attract, capture and pull success into our present.

Staying focused on what we have seen or experienced in our imagination is called a *waking dream*. Because it is easy to meditate on, it is effortless to rearrange the images in a waking dream, enabling us to construct future or even reconstruct past and present events to match our heart's desires.

The physical senses we use to discern possibilities are gathered through various tangible sensations and natural, instinctive impressions. Once we have determined the actions we desire to take place in our waking dream, we can state and outline their boundaries and the roles each person will play in carrying out our imagined desire or prayer. When every actor, heroine or heroic character has been assigned their function and responsibility, we can peacefully observe the screenplay we have created. We can visually realize and feel our desire coming to pass in our imagination.

There are a couple of steps we should incorporate in our spiritual disciplines that will help us in reconstructing or improving our future—resting in the Lord and expressing gratitude. If you recall, the final two chapters in the first volume of the *IMAGINE* series pertained to what it is to enter into and maintain rest. As we rest in the Lord, we can see and experience the waking dream as if the things we desire are actualizing in our imagination.

The actions in a waking dream or vision can be ordered and restructured by our focused attention. It creates a sustainable memory of the event in our mind's eye. This allows for it to be revisited again and again. As we seek the Holy Spirit for His wisdom, He will bring about the fulfillment of the waking dream.

God will give you everything you desire in life if you keep your love for Him in the most prominent position in all that you say and do. We are encouraged to continually seek first the Kingdom of God and His proceeding righteousness, constantly asking in God's names and nature in prayer, chasing after His right way of doing things and knocking on every door that leads to a different realm in God's mansions. When we invite the manifestation of All Things God to appear out of His spiritual rest, then All Things including those that are of less value and importance will be given to us in abundance (see Matthew 6:33).

All Things

The Being of All Things comprises All Things, the total entity. All power, all authority, all knowledge and all wisdom. This All Things Being contains the whole, entire and total amount, quantity or extent of every member or part of the whole number or sum of the positive, neutral and negative—the glorious and the traumatic—events in life. All Things contains the beginning and the end, the hope and the failures, the rest and the unrest, the good and the bad and the peace and the intolerance, of war and mob psychology, love and hate.

From Genesis to Revelation, All Things is mentioned 395 times. *And we know that All Things work together for good to those who love God, to those who are the called according to His purpose* (Romans 8:28). Are you prepared and able to love All Things? Can you love every person, race, tribe and culture?

I have given you All Things. The LORD had blessed Abraham in All Things; of All Things which I will give thee in commandment. All the hallowed, holy Things, All Things in your dwelling, All Things that you should do, as the LORD our God is in All Things for the abundance of All Things; and in want of All Things that we call upon Him for All Things (Genesis 24:1).

And you, by all means abstain from the accursed things, lest you become accursed when you take of the accursed things, and make the camp of Israel a curse, and trouble it (Joshua 6:18).

Behold, this day IAM going the way of all the earth. And you know in all your hearts and in all your souls that not one thing has failed of All the good Things which the LORD your God spoke concerning you. All have come to pass for you; not one word of them has failed. Therefore it shall come to pass, that as All the good Things have come upon you which the LORD your God promised you, so the LORD will bring upon you All harmful Things, until He has destroyed you from this good land which the LORD your God has given you (Joshua 23:14–15).

God has made with me an everlasting covenant, ordered in All Things and secure. For this is all my salvation and all my desire; will He not make it increase (2 Samuel 23:5)?

Life is about learning how to navigate and grow from All Things imaginable that come our way—the just and the unjust, the happy and the sad, the sorrow and the grief, the beautiful and the ugly. God is love! Are you able to embrace and love All Things?

LORD God of Abraham, Isaac, and Israel, let it be known this day that You are God in Israel and IAM Your servant, and that I have done All these Things at Your word (1 Kings 18:36).

*O LORD, for Your servant's sake, and according to Your own heart, You have done all this greatness, in making known All these great Things (*1 Chronicles 17:19).

Resting in the Lord enables us to rightly discern His desires for us. When we know what God wants, we can successfully define and express our objectives as we prayerfully describe and envision what we want. We create an imaginative event that entails all that we have asked for and sought to obtain by continually knocking on the door of opportunity. By seeing our God-given desires taking place in our restful conscious state, we can release our faith to believe it is done. There is no physical striving in this imaginative action, which is very similar to a waking state of sleep called the twilight zone. As we rest, while being conscious of the Lord and meditating on His will, Word and desire, His Spirit will open our eyes and direct our visionary paths.

> *The physical senses we use to discern possibilities are gathered through various, tangible sensations and natural, instinctive impressions.*

Expressing gratitude for the things we are shown in our imagination causes us to experience the feeling of an already-happened event or, what some would call, *déjà vu*. Living out our goals and ambitions in our imagination first will help us develop a successful strategy to manifest our desires in our waking life as well. Knowing the truth of the future gives us the freedom to manifest it in our present waking life (see John 8:32).

If we refuse to believe that something we desire is true and possible, we will not be able to see it in our imaginative dreams or visions. To seek to find or manifest something we hope is available in the outer world without first seeing and believing it in the mind's eye of our inner spiritual man is to seek, ask or knock in vain.

We can only give to or activate in others that which we are already conscious of possessing or being. To him who has been given, much more shall be given. For anyone to whom much is given, of him shall much be required; and to whom men have entrusted much, of him they will also require and demand all the more (see Luke 12:48).

CHAPTER TWO

Practicing the Presence of God

Before we can become familiar with and understand the workings of the realm of the Spirit, we must have knowledge of the essentialness of prayer. Therefore, I have included two chapters here about prayer and faith, even though these subjects will be further developed in the subsequent *IMAGINE* volume.

Prayer is a fundamental master key that unlocks access to all spiritual dimensions. Prayer is also absolutely necessary for the transformation from operating in the carnal to advancing in the Spirit. Prayer is essential to maintaining that higher state of being. Some may have a mistaken concept of prayer and its purpose. Some may consider prayer as a dutiful task or, at times, a somewhat boring obligation instead of an exciting, priceless privilege. Prayer is not just a vehicle used to communicate with God; it is a certain posture. It is the practicing of the presence of God.

The purpose of prayer is to lead us into imaginative rest, having received the answers we sought. In the habitation of resting in the Lord, we can place our entire trust in God, gain fresh vision and awaken our imagination to see our grandest destiny.

> *So now arise, O Lord God, and come into Your resting place, You and the ark of Your strength and power. Let Your priests, O Lord God, be clothed with salvation, and let Your saints,*

> *Your zealous ones, rejoice in good and in Your goodness* (2 Chronicles 6:41).

Prayer opens another facet or dimension of heaven in our spirit. Through prayer, our consciousness learns how to ascend into that heavenly place of rest. Once our soul enters into the obscure, unseen realm of the Spirit and rests there, we learn to continue to commune and abide with the Holy Spirit in prayer. When we are hidden from view and shrouded in His holy presence (in our imagination), we can sense, feel, hear or see the essence of the answer to our prayer that is in that secret place.

The coming of peace into our spirit lets us know that we have gained the needed revelation knowledge. Then we can see and embrace the visions that are shown and received. We can memorize everything about this mystifying realm. When the vision has imprinted on our spirit, we slowly descend back into our earthly vessel of consciousness. With the needed knowledge in hand, it is time to be sent out to communicate God's message. Endowed with God's power, we boldly disburse the demonstration of God's presence through the wisdom found in the revelatory vocal and power gifts of the Spirit.

> *Prayer is a fundamental master key that unlocks access to all spiritual dimensions.*

The art of prayer requires a disciplined, God-focused imagination. Always pray out of a thankful heart that is full with the Spirit of Love. Avoid prayers that are repetitive by nature, ones that are already written out or intellectually scripted by someone else. There is very little creative life in formulated scripts. *And when you pray, do not use vain repetitions or heap up wearisome phrases as the unbeliever does. For they think that they will be heard for their many words and elegant speeches* (Matthew 6:7). Prayer should be Spirit-inspired, Spirit-led and heartfelt.

The three essential components of prayer are faith, wisdom and understanding. Faith is defined as the assured confirmation of the title deed of the imaginary things we hope for, being the proof of things we do not currently see manifested in our life. Faith is the conviction of their reality. Our faith presently perceives the things we hope for as a real fact in our imagination, even though our hopes have not been revealed to the physical senses.

The saints and prophets of old gained a divine testimony of God's faithfulness. They obtained a good report because they trusted in and operated through a level of God-given, mountain-moving faith that ignited the power of faith in them. This faith birthed a holy fervor to see God's Kingdom manifested in a supernatural way every day.

Believing we have received our clearly-stated goals, feeling they are true, and then decreeing that thing will establish it. We don't receive answers to our prayer through force, might or power but by God's Spirit, we attract what we believe to be true. The Bible teaches that if we can believe for the things that we desire, seeing them as true and receiving those things as an already happened event, we can have them, because with God All Things are possible.

Wisdom is to accept the means to an end as a present reality so that the truth comes into our now. The imagination is the powerful force that awakens our heart to dream, to form godly desires that grow and bear fruit. But it is according to the measure of the substance of faith we possess that these God-given desires and fruits are formed.

By faith, we understand that the worlds during the successive ages were framed and fashioned, put in order and equipped for their intended purpose by the Word of God. What we see was not made out of things that are visible. The *God kind of faith* calls things that are not currently seen in the natural as though they were already fulfilled.

For those of us who believe in Christ, faith activates our ability to receive the divine promises that are already present resting in God. The Holy Spirit has offered us the ability to embrace the fullness of the promises found in His Word. We can enter into and experience Christ in another realm by resting in confident faith. God has placed eternity in the heart of our imagination because Christ dwells there. Yet we cannot discern the grandeur of God's creative works from their beginning or end. Everything we desire to be, everything we desire to achieve in life and all of the answers

The purpose of prayer is to lead us into imaginative rest.

we pray for already exist now as substance in the invisible dimensions of God's creative expanse.

The spiritually-disciplined man thinks of lovely, pure, holy things until he is able to transform his world by imagining and then feeling his desires are already real. He trades in the ashes of regret or past failures for the beauty found in the joy of his prayerful desire being granted.

Gazing into the invisible creative realms empowers us to imagine and see with the spiritual eyes of God. It is my belief that it is possible to see the beauties of the unseen world. Faith is the lens that brings the things that have always existed in the invisible realm into perfect view. In conjunction, the heart (imagination) is the sensory organ that perceives spiritual things.

> *But the Lord said to Samuel, "Do not look at his appearance or at his physical stature, because I have refused him. For the Lord does not see as man sees; for man looks at the outward appearance, but the Lord looks at the* (imagination) *heart"* (1 Samuel 16:7).

The imagination equips us with a powerful unction to create a fresh, futuristic vision. The vision that God gives us is able to guide us in constructing plans for the building of new concepts and support structures in the production of functional organizations. The imagination is used to form new ideas and reform old ideas. A healthy imagination causes us to rest in a creative peace that sustains the world around us.

> *Gazing into the invisible, creative realms empowers us to imagine and see with the spiritual eyes of God.*

By placing our faith in God, we can see the future. Faith manifests the invisible designs we have seen projected in the images of our heart. By focusing the 'mind's eye' upon the vague images of our imagination, we learn how to concentrate in order to give them expressed clarity. We gain understanding that perfects them in their function so that they can be transferred into the now moments of our reality!

We are transformed into the image of God by taking possession of a faith-filled, righteous state of consciousness. This transpires when we realize we already are who Jesus says we are and that which we desire to be. Imaginative faith places our confidence, loyal allegiance and strong convictions in a higher place in God when our complete trust is resting in God alone. We possess a firm belief in His creative power, even when there is no logical basis of proof.

Faith manifests the invisible designs we have seen projected in the images of our heart.

Imaginative faith is placing our trust and belief in God and in the fidelity (sincere intentions) of a person or thing to act in good assurance. When we live according to that kind of faith, we, like Moses, can speak to a rock and the waters of revelation will gush forth to quench the thirst of a whole nation of desert wanderers (see Numbers 20:8). This kind of imaginative faith is added to our own faith, so we can access the unlimited faith of God. The more of God's characteristic and attributes we take onto ourselves the more we are transformed into His image and likeness.

Imaginative faith empowers us to believe and physically respond to the mental visions of the imagination. We yield to and follow what we have seen in God's domain by moving with their co-existing, expressive feelings that our sustained prayerful state has produced in our spirit. *Therefore, I say to you, whatever things you ask when you pray, believe that you receive them, and you will have them* (Mark 11:24).

Prayer cannot attract to us what we want or for what we ask if we do not believe it is true or possible. Never entertain, not even for a brief moment, that there is a possibility of failure. If we focus on empowering the natural feelings of the body or the negative attitudes of the soul's mind, will or emotions, they will always dissipate the illusive Spirit's triumphant cloud by trampling it into the ground.

To be successful in prayer, one must learn how to turn off the five natural, reasoning senses. Instead of moving in the natural, carnal realm, learn to activate, use and develop your ability to receive revelation knowledge through the five spiritual senses (sight, taste and smell and the sensations of what you feel and the sounds you hear). Prayer should be a spiritual encounter of reality that includes becoming a holy habitation for God. In this place of intimate surrender, we enter into dialogue with the living God, who we see, hear, feel and taste by experiencing all these different aspects of His unending love.

The spirit is the true sensory organ of the body. When the human spirit is connected with the Holy Spirit, He leads, guides and directs us into all truth. When truth is seen, heard or felt, it is then actualized through faith. In prayer, our faith is turned into sight so that what and who we see can be brought into our natural world. *So, God created man in His own image, in the image of God He created him; male and female He created them* (Genesis 1:27).

Prayer is futile if you allow yourself to entertain carnal reasoning. Never slip into the rote memory of head knowledge or permit your consciousness to rule by interjecting its judgmental opinions. Your mindfulness, doubt and cognitive perceptions will always contradict the prayers, focused faith and creative desires of your imaginative subconscious. Do not allow your physical senses or carnal reasoning to negate the vision of what you have seen by faith. Without faith, it is impossible to please God. Faith without action is dead. Embrace the powerful visual sights and feelings that faith releases in order to move forward and receive your declarations in prayer.

Jesus is moved to action by faith.

> *There were two blind men* (unimaginative people) *who followed Jesus crying out, "Son of David, have mercy on us!" The blind men* (people without vision) *came to Jesus where Jesus asked them, "Do you believe that I am able to do this?" They both replied, "Yes, Lord!" Then Jesus touched their eyes* (vision) *and said, "According to your faith* (the measure of your imagination) *let it be to you." And immediately their eyes* (vision) *were opened! As Jesus was leaving, they brought to Him a man, mute* (someone who does not speak the Word of God) *and demon possessed* (controlled by fear, wrong thoughts and evil images). *After the demons were cast out, the mute spoke. And the multitudes marveled, "It was never seen like this in Israel"* (Matthew 9:27–33)*!*

The unimaginative person without any vision, who did not previously believe or speak the Word but was controlled by fear, doubt and unbelief, finally saw Jesus (the Light of the World) and apprehended faith to imagine what life would be like if he spoke the truth.

Jesus was moved with compassion. He went about all the cities and villages teaching and preaching the gospel of the Kingdom of God. He healed every sickness and every disease among the people. Jesus was successful because His focus was on the Kingdom's power of love. *Remember, "It is not by might nor by power, but by My Spirit." says the Lord of hosts* (Zechariah 4:6).

Prayer can only draw into your presence that which you picture and are already conscious of believing, being or possessing. Therefore, prayer is a skillful art that you must adequately develop. Look to see what God is doing, listen for His wisdom, and then actively assume the posture of becoming what He desires. Continue to sustain that identity to be who God created you to be.

Imaginative faith empowers us to physically respond to the mental visions of the imagination.

God is all-knowing, and He always has our best in mind. Typically, we resist change simply because it requires us to change. But if we do not seek God, pray and see what He has in store for us, we will never become the person He has designed us to be. Taking on a new identity is easy when we see and know who we were created to be in Christ. To see is to be, if we will imagine, pray and then say what we see and be what we say. Vision comes to give us a new blueprint so that we can grow up into in Christ. All we need, want, hope for or will ever desire to be is found in Christ.

We take on a new identity that is full of compassion by feeling God's love, taking in His love as our own and then actively portraying the loving image of Jesus. Through the substance of faith, everything in the world that was hoped for was imagined, framed, created and became the evidence of the thing not yet seen.

When we sense, hear and see Jesus' love, we experience God in a way that empowers us to become love. By mirroring the person of Christ, we become the loving, caring person Christ designed us to be.

> *Let this mind be in you which was also in Christ Jesus, who, being in the form of God, did not consider it robbery to be equal with God, but made Himself of no reputation, taking the form of a bondservant, and coming in the likeness of men* (Philippians 2:5–7).

Jesus knew and confessed that He and His Father were one (see John 10:31). As Believers, we must become one in spirit and in truth with God and His love. The world will know and recognize Jesus because of our love one for another. *Most assuredly, I say to you, he who believes as I believe and has the same type of faith as, the works that I do he will do also; and greater works than these he will do, because I go to My Father* (John 14:12).

Becoming one with God is being as God manifested on earth in the flesh. Always celebrate God's goodness by giving thanks for and rejoicing at having received what you have asked for in prayer. Thanksgiving brings an increase and multiplication of receptivity and creativity. Then proficiently apply the answers you received in prayer by bringing them into your present conscious state.

Prayer should take place in a relaxed, passive state in order to activate the imagination to see, watch and follow the actions of Christ Jesus (the Christ consciousness) within us saying, "IAM the beginning and the end. The IAM has sent Me, so be still and know that IAM God. IAM the Lord. There is no God, except Me." This activates our imagination to see picture images. We hear and receive creative thoughts. When we become one with the Lord our God, Christ gives us the power and wisdom to carry out the things we see, hear and believe as true. If we do not take on and demonstrate the full image of who we know and believe God to be, we ignore, neglect, discard or take those characteristic portions of His names in vain.

> *Answers to prayer are waiting for us to discover them in the glorious realms of the Spirit.*

The spiritual body of our imagination moves beyond the natural, current realm of reality to connect us with the fluid realms of the dimensions of time—past, present or future. Each of these time dimensions are continually flowing, so they hold part of the knowledge, experience, solution, wisdom or power that is able to grant us the answers to our prayer requests. Everything we could ever need, desire or pray for has already been answered by God's infinite intelligence. *But there is a vital force a spirit of intelligence in man, and the breath of the Almighty gives men understanding* (Job 32:8).

We must be attuned to the Spirit of God so that we know which dimension of time (past, present or future) or eternity to tap into in order to retrieve God's desire for us at that moment. Jesus is the proceeding Word. He is always active, stirring and advancing in wisdom to release new revelation and spiritual upgrades.

Answers to prayer are waiting for us to discover them in the glorious realms of the Spirit. The solution to every problem is hidden within the question. We only need to imagine it, create it, pray to see it, have faith to believe it, stay focused and then decree the answer in order to obtain and sustain our new identity. The Holy Spirit is resident within us and is waiting in the realms of glory for us to connect to Him. He wants us to ask for His wise answers. Active, intentional faith that produces eternal results is always moving in the miraculous realm of NOW!

CHAPTER THREE

Prayer Activation

Now that you have learned the importance of prayer and how to activate it, allow me to take you through the process of drawing the answers to your prayers into your waking realm! Like attempting anything new, the first go at this may require a notable amount of time and effort. The art of quieting your industrious mind that is accustomed to operating in high volumes of noise and busyness may take some discipline. However, as you continue to practice this type of imaginative prayer, it will become more easygoing as your thought processes shift.

> First, find a quiet, secluded place free of distractions. Sit or recline in a comfortable position, and close your eyes to enter into rest.
>
> Take a few deep breaths in, and slowly exhale all of your stress, fear and anxiety. Remain stationary. Intentionally relax your body completely. Silence the thoughts of your mind. Let go of all physical, emotional and mental activity.
>
> Begin with forgiveness. Forgive and release yourself. Then forgive and release anyone else who comes to mind.
>
> Repent from any wrongdoings of which you are aware. Remove all criticisms, negative thoughts, judgments and harmful ideas or suggestions. Replace them with thoughts of love, mercy, grace,

well-being, gentleness, kindness, blessings, welfare and prosperity. If you have difficulty, try reading or quoting Scripture that pertains to renewing your mind with positive thoughts.

Give thanks. Affirm that your position is centered in Christ. Tell the Holy Spirit how much you need, want, desire and love Him.

Ask the Holy Spirit to show you an image of His beautiful face so you can adore and worship Him. Be patient. Rest in His presence and warm embrace. Wait on Him to reveal His plans.

Once you receive the new vision He has for you, focus on His higher purposes and longings for your life as they continue to come into view. Imagine pictures and visions of what you want to be, do, acquire or achieve. Let your imagination flow freely without restraint.

Focus your attention on them until they become clear. Feel them with all of your senses until they become a living reality that you can see, breath in, touch, feel, embrace, take on, fully experience and encounter.

Listen for the Holy Spirit to give the thoughts of your heart the wisdom that is needed to prophesy the ability to obtain this new state of being.

This can be an exciting experience, so talk to and calm your body, if needed, until it is in a state of peaceful rest again.

Now activate your spirit to rise up through the emotion of love within your soul. Prayerfully attract peace, harmony, love, joy and the gentleness of the Holy Spirit's embrace. Remember to activate the fruit of the Spirit. Be patient and long-suffering with yourself. Be self-controlled.

Prophesy a higher caliber of quality people you desire to come into your life.

Surround yourself with people of integrity and godly character, and everything you touch will be blessed and will become golden and fruitful. Call into being those who possess a loyal character and who are reliable, honest, full of uprightness, intelligent and have acquired the necessary skills to prosper your life.

Agree with any changes the Holy Spirit shows you that need to take place. Remind your subconscious to let go of the old identity and habitual ways of doing things. Put on the fresh, new identity. Become the person you are envisioning by feeling, obeying and fulfilling your God-given desires.

When you see yourself in this new light, know that your prayer has been answered.

Continue to behold the vision of your new image as you gently emerge from this prayerful state. Believe you have been changed and transformed into a new image of Christ.

Awaken as a new person ready to live your life as this new creature in Christ. Shed your old, dry, stiff wineskin. Take on the new, flexible, supple, elastic wineskin that expands and yields to God's new vision for you.

Journal your experience; write down the vision of your new identity. The writing of your spiritual encounters helps to bring it out of the realm of the Spirit and into the natural realm, which is tangible. Recording the vision plants it in your soul so that the new identity can take root, grow, mature and bring forth a multiplied harvest in your waking world.

Receive and activate all of these new spiritual gifts, because they have already become a living part of you. Hold onto these new abilities by possessing, initiating and setting into motion the new identity found in these visionary images and ideas. *For the gifts and the calling of God are irrevocable* (Romans 11:29).

This type of visionary prayer declaration can be used to draw *anything* into our waking realm—an ideal mate, the model business partner or the perfect career opportunity—the ability to create wealth, sell property or manifest the miracle or healing power of Christ in your body or in someone you love.

When you are praying for a healing or miracle to manifest, be sure to visualize the person in a whole, healthy state of wellness. Never picture them as weak, diseased, sick, halt or lame and confined in a hospital bed with tubes or machines hooked up to them. All of these vain imaginations must be bound, cast down and defeated. Pray until you can see that person happy and rejoicing, because they are strong and totally healed.

We will believe, speak, create and manifest what we see in our imagination. Therefore, remain focused on producing life more abundantly. Never accept, agree with or dwell on a negative image or situation. It is the thief who comes and injects images that kill, steal and destroy life, not God.

When you are praying, it is important that you do it for the purpose of God's kingdom advancement, not just to amass personal wealth or self-aggrandizement. *And when you do ask, you do not receive, because you ask with wrong motives, that you may squander it on your pleasures* (James 4:3).

Prayerfully consider God's wise answers. Decree that you already have the things you need. God will release, highlight and distribute the already existing answers to your prayers. Faith draws the answers to our prayers out of the Spirit realm's incubator. Answers to prayer are established on earth when they reside in and manifest through our earthen vessel, the body. When we are touched by the presence of God, we are never the same. *Then He touched their eyes, saying, "According to your faith let it be to you"* (Matthew 9:29).

When you are praying for a healing or miracle to manifest, be sure to visualize the person in a whole, healthy state of wellness.

We have all been given a different measure of faith. When Jesus touches us, that quantity of faith is extended. Our spiritual eyes are given the ability to see everything in a more splendid way. The visionary sight we are given includes the magnificent way we finally see the amazing amount of potential that was hidden within. The more of a positive image that we receive and believe is possible, the more we are able to give in the service of God and man. *Every man shall give as he is able, according to the blessing of the Lord your God which He has given you* (Deuteronomy 16:17).

When we trust in the Lord with all of our heart, Christ delivers, strengthens and redeems us. God's Word is proven; it has a powerful, transforming, effective conclusion for all who believe and do not lean on their own limited understanding. *Blessed is the man who makes the Lord his trust, and does not respect or listen to the proud, nor such as turn aside to lies* (Psalm 40:4).

CHAPTER FOUR

Realm of the Spirit

By entering into imaginative rest, we are able to learn how to use our imagination so that we can be still and know that He is God. When we know God, we can hear, believe, see and follow Him by placing our entire trust in Him. There is a promise that remains of entering His rest. So let us fear the Lord and mix our faith with the Word of God so that we do not fall short of manifesting rest (see Hebrews 4).

The entering and unfolding of God's Word gives light unto our path. It gives understanding, spiritual discernment and comprehension of truth to the simple. The Holy Spirit shines light upon the path of those who love Jesus. *God forms the light and creates darkness, He makes a nation be at peace, and He creates physical evil or calamity; He is the Lord, who does all these things* (Isaiah 45:7).

We who have believed do enter into that supernatural, God-given rest. *For thus said the Lord God, the Holy One of Israel: "In returning to Me and resting in Me, you shall be saved; in quietness and in trusting, confidence shall be your strength"* (Isaiah 30:15).

In rest, we do not take random actions or try to force something to happen by our own efforts. We actively wait in expectant prayer. We love, worship and adore God. Here in the realm of rest, we can embrace the kind of peace that is only found by those who have their being in His divine presence. Every time we see Christ and recognize Him coming in a new way, if we will enter into that peace and maintain that restful expression of Him, we are instantly conformed into that portion of His image.

When Jesus comes into our consciousness, the presence of His glory envelops us, transforming us into His image. Once that transformation takes place, we can maintain His likeness by staying clothed in the robe of righteousness. God's righteousness is manifested when we continue to live in right standing with God. *And now, little children, abide in Him, that when He appears, we may have confidence and not be ashamed before Him at His coming* (1 John 2:28).

Jesus is the transformational door that leads us to our spiritual rebirth, divine revelation and godly wisdom.

As the Holy Spirit trains us to enter in and out of the different realms of the Spirit, we learn how to believe, see, touch, taste, hear and feel in that particular spiritual realm. In order to bypass the five natural senses that try to keep us restrained to the earthly realm, we must continue to commune with the Holy Spirit to learn how to move in those spiritual dimensions. To move beyond the false veil of no into the true and unlimited yes of God, we must be determined to surrender to the shaking that demolishes all of our old supports and structures.

By agreeing with God's higher will for our life, we, like Jesus in the Garden of Gethsemane, are saying, "Not my will but Thine be done!" To maintain a spiritual presence before the Lord, we must lay aside the old man. In order to be renewed in the spirit of our mind, we must do away with all of the former man's old forms. The Holy Spirit will inspire us to dream again, transcend earthly limitations and ascend and soar through the open door into heavenly places.

Jesus has gone before to prepare a place for us in a higher dimension, where He continually dwells. Jesus shared that He has many prepared mansions (states of being) in His Father's house for us to access. Jesus is the transformational door that leads us to our spiritual rebirth, divine revelation and godly wisdom. Jesus gives us access to all of His heavenly knowledge that prepares us to reach our destiny. Jesus is the door of entrance. He gives the Believer access to every spiritual realm, ascending levels, rooms, houses, chambers, courtrooms, mansions and every heavenly dimension. Jesus is the eternal Way that delivers us from natural causes. He leads and guides us into the depths of all truth.

There are many appearings, comings, goings and manifestations of the Lord Jesus. He visits us and lives in our imagination (home, temple or mansion) that is housed within our earthly body. *Nor will people say, "Look! Here the Kingdom of God is! or, "See, the Kingdom of God is there!" For behold, the Kingdom of God is within you, in your hearts* (imagination) *and among you, surrounding you* (Luke 17:21).

Before we can ascend into heavenly mansions, we must first recognize Christ living largely within us. As our spirits mature, we continue to gain revelation in order to ascend to higher spiritual levels by entering into more powerful mansions.

To achieve a specific, predetermined desire or state of being, we must access the much larger, four-dimensional realm of the Spirit. The four-dimensional realm, which is intangible, is explored by using the concentrated powers of our imagination. The spiritual fourth dimension is a creative realm that is not known by touch or measured by length, width, breadth or height. Because a dimension is a substance of obscure things, it is also a hidden element, a concealed component or varied facet that is hoped for. Therefore, a dimension is not just a simple abstract point on a line; it is an unseen, multifaceted and impalpable realm of existence.

We are able to measure spiritual dimensions by the amount of time that we are able to believe, see, enter into them and sustain their appearance—also by the amount of time that we are able to glean revelation, hear wisdom or access knowledge before their disappearance. We determine their lifespan by our ability to concentrate the focus of our single-minded thoughts and prayers on a specific outcome.

We must spiritually ascertain how to modify and enhance our existing opportunities.

In the fourth dimension, our imagination highlights the undetectable, invisible shadows and impressions. Our spirit reflects on gaining revelation knowledge and divine understanding of our dreams and visions. Whenever we extract our inner images to externalize our inner concepts (by continuing to focus on a desired outcome for an undetermined amount of time), we are able to increase both the space and the clarity of that particular four-dimensional reality.

If we continue to sustain our focus in real time, we are able to rework, increase and possess our four-dimensional future. We must spiritually ascertain how to modify and enhance our existing opportunities. We ask God for His wisdom and seek His face for understanding. Then we must be willing to choose the highest potential or destiny offered in the fourth dimension. We must take on a larger spiritual identity that is centered in resurrecting the power of Christ within us before we can realize the fullness of our destiny in our solid, three-dimensional world.

There are immeasurable mansions to be discovered in the spiritual realm with various keys that unlock each dimension. When I speak of keys, I am referring to numerous ways, means and methods to the Kingdom of God, channels formed by Christ's agencies that unlock the doors of heavenly access.

Keys to the Kingdom

Hearts that are focused on the Kingdom of God coming to earth create movement in God's throne room. The keys to the Kingdom unlock the doors of heavenly access. *I will give you the keys of the kingdom of heaven; and whatever you bind on earth shall have been bound in heaven, and whatever you loose on earth shall have already been loosed in heaven* (Matthew 6:19). This passage confirms the necessity that we believe, see, hear, survey and track with whatever is presently occurring in heaven.

> *A dimension is not just a simple abstract point on a line; it is an unseen, multifaceted and impalpable realm of existence.*

We learn to follow heaven's lead by doing on earth what we see the Father doing in heaven. The keys of God connect us to heavenly access. The keys to the Kingdom of God give us kingdom ownership and greater authority as joint heirs in Christ. Faith (a master key) opens the double doors so that we can break out of the narrow limitations of the past. As we continue to seek God with all of our heart, we move forward with strategic, godly plans for restructuring our ability to follow through into the new, boldly leaving our past in the past.

I have already mentioned a few of the keys that unlock access to the Kingdom and will continue to refer to particular keys throughout the *IMAGINE* series. There are far too many to specifically list, but I will include several of the *master keys* here so that you can have an idea of what I am meaning.

Master keys include (but are not limited to): the nine fruits of the Spirit; the Seven Spirits of God; living promises of the Word of God; the names, characteristics and attributes of God; the imagination; visions; dreams; prayer; prophecy; decrees and declarations; faith; wisdom; revelation knowledge; word of knowledge; spiritual intelligence; divine strategy; desiring God's will; the keys of David.

> *The keys of David empower us to become whatever God needs us to be at any moment.*

Some keys shut, lock or seal destructive doors. Other keys empower us to unlock and open doors that give us access to blessings, healing, revelation knowledge, wisdom and a fresh, prosperous vision for the future. When one vision is completed, it is evaluated by heaven to determine the measure of our success. A new vision quickly emerges to inspire greatness within our being. Otherwise, without a fresh vision, we would lack direction, fester in boredom, languish and eventually perish.

The keys of David and the mighty foundational Rock, Jesus, proclaimed in the gospel message of salvation are all necessary to take down the giants of opposition. These diabolical giants come in all forms of fear and religious and political spirits (for example, the Queen of Heaven and Jezebel, abortion, murder, poverty, disease and infirmity).

The keys of David empower us to be kings who reign in God's Kingdom. We become psalmists, worshippers and the friends and lovers of God. We learn to be shepherds who protect the flocks of God against the devil and the adversarial lions, bears and giants. Kings are businessmen and leading women who rule, reign and dominate the business sectors, corporate America, stock markets and all forms of commerce.

The keys of David empower us to become whatever God needs us to be at any moment. IAM a warrior, IAM a deliverer, IAM a multinational corporate professional or IAM a president of a business conglomerate, because

IAM a giant slayer! God's Word will not return void. Wherever we send God's Word, it causes our plans to succeed. We triumph as the head of every organization.

> *The keys of David open doors that no one can shut and shuts doors that no one can open. I know your deeds. Behold, I have put before you an open door which no one can shut, because you have a little power, and have kept My Word, and have not denied My name. Behold, I will cause those of the synagogue of Satan, who say that they are Jews and are not, but lie—I will make them come and bow down at your feet, and make them know that I have loved you* (Revelation 3:7–9).

Faith is the magnetic gate that brings eternity into time! Faith releases the *now* of God that has already been predetermined in heaven. Faith is a heavenly connective powerline that flows into and through us that gives heaven an access point into the earth. Believers arise with keys in their hand to unlock greater doors of opportunity. These prospective doors expand God's influence according to the measure of faith we have to prophesy, pray and decree faith-filled statements, to believe for God's kingdom advancement. The measure of faith and confidence we have in God will determine the measure of faith and self-confidence we possess. Your power and authority are linked with your level of faith.

Faith is a master key that creates imagination and unlocks our internal doors and spiritual gateways. Faith releases our dreams from their period of gestation (reference to the six days of focused prayer before entering into rest), where time has been holding them inside our imagination's incubation chamber. Faith gives our dreams the ability to flourish, grow and be birthed. Faith produces the wind under our wings that gives lift to our dreams, empowering them to be set free, take flight and soar to the surface. Faith empowers us to live out the grand schemes of our dreams.

Faith is a master key that creates and unlocks our internal doors and spiritual gateways.

The radiant presence of God dwelling within us opens amazing doors of opportunity. As new creatures in Christ, we are able to grow and change in numerous, positive ways, which causes us to blossom as we move throughout our life.

The Master Door

Although there are many keys, there is only one door—Jesus. He is the door to every dimension. Jesus used several illustrations to communicate the spiritual doors and gates, but people did not understand the mysteries He spoke about.

> *Most assuredly, I say to you, he who does not enter the sheepfold by the door, but climbs up over the fence or crawls in some other way, rather than walking through the door or gate the same is a thief, vandal or a robber. But He who enters openly by the door is the Shepherd of the sheep. To Him the doorkeeper opens, and the sheep hear His voice; and He calls His own sheep by name and leads them out. And when all the sheep have been gathered, He brings out His own sheep, He goes before them; and the sheep follow Him, for they know His voice. Yet they will by no means follow a stranger, but will flee from him, for they do not know the voice of strangers.*
>
> *I AM the Gate or Door for the sheep. All those others are up to no good—sheep stealers, every one of them. But the sheep didn't listen to them. I AM the Gate! I AM the only Door! Anyone who enters in and goes through Me will be saved and cared for—they will experience spiritual liberty to freely go in and out, and find pasture. A thief is only there to steal and kill and destroy. I came so they can have really abundant, eternal life, more and better life than they ever dreamed of. I AM the Good Shepherd* (John 10:1–10).

The Good Shepherd puts the sheep before Himself, and He sacrifices Himself if necessary. A hired hand is not a real shepherd. Because he does not own them, the sheep are of no matter to a hired hand. If he sees a wolf coming, he runs for it and leaves the sheep to be ravaged and scattered by the wolf. A hired hand is not invested in the sheep's well-being, as he is only in it for the money. Jesus is most certainly not a hired hand.

> *I am the Good Shepherd. I know My own sheep, and My own*

> *sheep know Me. In the same way, the Father knows Me, and I know the Father. I put the sheep before Myself, sacrificing My very life if necessary. You need to know that I have other sheep all over the world in addition to those in this pen. I need to gather and bring them too. They'll also recognize My voice. Then it will be one flock, with one Shepherd. This is why the Father loves Me: because I freely lay down My life. And so, I am free to take it up again. No one takes My life from Me. I lay it down of My own free will. I have the right to lay it down; I also have the power to take it up again. I received this authority personally from My Father's command* (John 10:11–18).

There is only one proper, legal way to enter into the spiritual realms—Jesus! Salvation through the blood of Jesus gives the Believer the right to enter into the Kingdom of God.

CHAPTER FIVE

Doors to Dimensions

For the next few moments, please allow me take you through a visual tour (in your imagination).

> Imagine a doorway in your home, office or church. Now imagine it as a massive door that leads into a magnificent castle or a parallel spiritual dimension. The door is closed and locked; you are unable to gain entrance.
>
> Now imagine you have been given the specific key especially formed and designed to unlock the tumblers in that particular lock. Place your key in the lock. Turn the key to the right, press your thumb down on the handle's paddle until it clicks and push the door wide open.
>
> Imagine you see a vast space without any walls or barriers. Envision the entire broadness (height, length and depth) of the expansive space that is now before you. You have unlimited possibilities available to you in that immense, infinite, immeasurable place. This is the beauty of the spiritual realm. You can imagine, design, believe for, see and create anything you want, need or desire.
>
> Before you enter the room, notice the secure, supportive, protective frame that surrounds the door. People say be-

> cause a door frame is a secure structure, it is one of the safest places to seek shelter during an earthquake. Door frames easily support the weight of many different styles of doors, no matter how heavy, thin, tall or thick or what type of materials they are made of. The threshold of the frame is not very deep; you can easily step across it with one stride.
>
> Now inch your way under the narrow space supporting the door (doorway), and stand on the threshold. Observe the width and depth of the door frame. In my home, the various framed doorways range from seven to twelve inches. When we visit a friend or neighbor, we do not stand at or dwell in the doorway. We are invited inside to visit. No one stays or camps out in the doorway for long. It is only an entry point where you gain vision of where and what you are about to step into.

As we stand in God's presence at the gate of every entrance, we are transformed into the image and take on the likeness of God that is manifested in the next dimension. We are granted a new measure of power and authority in order to rule, reign and take dominion in that sphere. We have the ability to bind, cast down and remove any strongman or antichrist structure.

When the cherubim stood still, the wheels stood still, and when one was lifted up, the other lifted itself up, for the spirit of the living creature was in them (Ezekiel 10:17).

Therefore, we can enter in and flow as one with the Spirit of God that resides there. We must have the veils removed from our face so that we can see how to enter in and experience or mirror that different level of glory. *But we all, with unveiled face, beholding as in a mirror the glory of the Lord, are being transformed into the same image from glory to glory, just as by the Spirit of the Lord* (2 Corinthians 3:18).

Spiritual doorways are a short transition space that allows us to gain access to an altered space or dimension, a diverse room, a changed chamber or another transitional hallway that exists beyond the framed entry point. If I am given the option of standing restrained in the limited, narrow dimension of the doorway or of stepping into the fullness of another dimension or room to believe, see and experience all that is available, naturally I would choose the unlimited exposure. Wouldn't you?

Sadly, most Believers never venture into the deep things of God. They never mature or grow past the entry level of getting into the door of salvation. *However, we speak spiritual wisdom among those who are mature, yet not the wisdom of this age, nor of the rulers of this age, who are coming to nothing* (1 Corinthians 2:6).

Most people spend their entire life at the starting gate, waiting for someone to give them their approval or permission to live their dream. *Brethren, do not be children in understanding; however, in malice be babes, but in understanding be mature* (1 Corinthians 14:20). When they pray, they do not receive the answers to their prayers. This is because they never use their God-given imagination to enter into the vast Kingdom of God (exercise their faith to carry them beyond the shallows) to apprehend the depths of wisdom and grace God has reserved for them to find.

We must transition into spiritual maturity. We must be willing to imagine our possibilities, create our opportunities, feel and believe they are true and be self-disciplined enough to exercise our faith to go beyond our current boundaries

---

Beyond

Where have you been?
"Beyond!"
Beyond where? What?
"Beyond myself, into new
Dimensions, unexplored;
Mind-expanding, spirit soaring,
Experiencing well beyond beyond;
Beyond perceived reality into
And beyond imagination."

Keat Wade 02/26/18 (17 Sh'vat 5778)

Our Father is continuously moving us—fully tied to Him—forward and upward, ever-expanding and consolidating us in one fluid flow that we often only see in hindsight with foresight.

When we know what we want and ask for it, we are able to control our subconscious thoughts. We are able to rule, reign and take dominion in any sphere of authority that we enter. When we correctly discern our beliefs and join our faith and imagination together, we can create keys that allow us entrance into vast, new realms of access. We ask until permission is granted. We seek until we find, and we knock until it is opened to us. But once we ask, seek and find, we must not doubt! We must believe the truth and emerge from prayer knowing it is done!

We must transition into spiritual maturity.

Paul explained spiritual maturity this way:

> *IAM not there yet so don't think that I have already attained or become perfected; but I press on, to gain anything and everything the Anointed One, Jesus, that I may lay hold of that for which Christ Jesus has also stored up for me. Nothing will stand in my way, because Jesus has held onto me, and He won't let me go. Brothers and sisters, as I said, I know I have not arrived; but there's one thing IAM doing: IAM leaving my old life and fleshly ways behind, putting everything on the line for this. IAM reaching forward to those things which are ahead. IAM sprinting toward the only goal that counts: to cross the beginning line master the in between and then cross the finish, to win the prize. I press toward the goal for the prize of ascending in the upward call of God in Christ Jesus. I hear God's call to resurrection life which is found exclusively in Jesus the Anointed.*
>
> *All of us who are mature have this same thought of mind; and if in anything you have a different attitude or think otherwise, God will reveal even this mystery to you. For now, let's hold on to the degree that we have already attained, to what we have been shown, let us walk by the same rule, let us be of the same mind as Christ and keep in step with these spiritual principles and teachings.*
>
> *Imitate me, brothers and sisters, and look around to those al-*

> *ready following the example we have set. I have warned you before and now say again through my tears that we have many enemies—people who reject the cross of the Anointed. They are ruled by their bellies, their glory comes by shame, and their minds are fixed on the things of this world. They are doomed. But we are citizens of heaven, exiles on earth waiting eagerly for a Liberator, our Lord Jesus the Anointed, to come and transform these humble, earthly bodies into the form of His glorious body by the same power that brings All Things under His control* (Philippians 3:12–21).

We begin the process of becoming a Believer by first finding Jesus, for He is the only door to eternity. Jesus, being the Spirit of Truth, is the narrow door and guiding pathway that leads to a vast eternal life. Those who find spiritual truth also find eternal life. To know Christ Jesus, we begin by knowing the living Christ that continually dwells within us. *For if when we were enemies we were reconciled to God through the death of His Son, much more, having been reconciled, we shall be saved by His life* (Romans 5:10).

To know Christ Jesus, we begin by knowing the living Christ that continually dwells within us.

The Bible tells us that we cannot even find Jesus on our own. The Father has to draw us to His Son. *No one can come to Me unless the Father who sent Me draws him; and I will raise him up at the last day* (John 6:44). The Father gives us His favor and draws us to Jesus in the realm of the Spirit.

Jesus is the master door that begins the process of walking out our eternal life with fear and trembling.

> *With enthusiasm work out cultivate, carry out to the goal, and fully complete your own salvation with reverence and awe and trembling. Distrust your own strength with serious caution, tenderness of conscience, watchfulness against temptation, timidly shrinking from whatever might offend God and discredit the name of Christ. For it is God who is all the while effectually at work in you energizing and creating in you the power and desire, both to will and to work for His good pleasure and*

satisfaction and delight (Philippians 2:12–13).

As we mature, we enter a new door. When we graduate from one level, we ascend to a parallel place that offers us new doors to explore.

Each door mirrored throughout the realms of eternity represent a subsequent place where we start fresh with a new beginning. A spiritual door is a stepping off point. Before we can graduate to another higher entry-level or enter a new door, we must have studied to show ourselves approved by mastering the elementary things on previous levels. Each door we are able to open exposes us to a new place, region, state or mansion that demands our full spiritual attention to discover the treasures buried there. *O Lord, by these things men live; and in all these things is the life of my spirit; so, You will restore me and make me live* (Isaiah 38:16).

Jesus has gone before us to prepare a place of abundance for us in the Father's spiritual house. The Father's house is full of gifts, anointings, glorious mansions, states of being, creative dimensions and expanding galaxies. When Jesus ascended on high, He led the captive into their reward, and in that place of liberty, He gave gifts to men.

Your Father, who is in heaven, gives good things to those who enter into His presence to ask Him! Once the gifts are given, they are never taken away, for the gifts and callings of God are irrevocable. To each one of us, grace was given according to the measure of Christ's gift, for there are diversities of gifts, but the same Spirit. The gifts that we each receive differ according to the grace that is given to us and the manner in which we use them.

Each door we are able to open exposes us to a new place, region, state or mansion that demands our full spiritual attention to discover the treasures buried there.

Phillip experienced a geographic transportation from a barren place when he was propelled into the Spirit and instantly traveled over forty miles down the desert road to the city of Azotus. *Now when they came up out of the water, the Spirit of the Lord caught Philip away so that the eunuch saw him no more; and he went on his way rejoicing* (Acts 8:39-40).

Apostle Paul experienced being immediately translated from the earthly realm to the spiritual paradise of heaven:

> *I will come to visions and revelations of the Lord: I know a man in Christ who fourteen years ago—whether in the body I do not know, or whether out of the body I do not know, God knows—such a one was caught up to the third heaven. And I know such a man—whether in the body or out of the body I do not know, God knows—how he was caught up into Paradise and heard inexpressible words, which it is not lawful for a man to utter* (2 Corinthians 12:1-4).

The ability to travel in and to know how to operate the realm of the Spirit has long been a mystery to mankind because we dwell in the lower natural, earthly plane of carnal knowledge most of the time. To flow in the Spirit, we must learn how to surrender our will and desire to immediately trust and obediently follow the Holy Spirit. *Then the Spirit entered me and set me on my feet, and spoke with me and said to me: "Go, shut yourself inside your house"* (Ezekiel 3:24).

We must be able to discern the comings and goings of the Lord and His spiritual agents—beasts, lights, winds, angels, cherubim, seraphim, wheels, Merkavah, living creatures—and the anointings and functions of a myriad of other heavenly beings.

> *Wherever the Spirit wanted to go, they went, because there the Spirit went; and the wheels were lifted together with them, for the Spirit of the living creatures was in the wheels. When those went, these went; when those stood, these stood; and when those were lifted up from the earth, the wheels were lifted up together with them, for the spirit of the living creature was in the wheels* (Ezekiel 1:20–21).

The human body is so fearfully and wonderfully made that the Trinity Eternal can reside within us. *Brethren, the grace of our Lord Jesus Christ be with your spirit. Amen* (Galatians 6:18). All three persons of the Godhead dwell in their fullness within the spirit of the Believer. It is our job to discover each of them and recognize their voices, touch and mannerisms. We must learn how to cooperate with each of the natures, characteristics and manifestations. *The grace of the Lord Jesus Christ, and the love of God, and the communion of the Holy Spirit be with you all. Amen* (2 Corinthians 13:14).

The Kingdom of God and the kingdom of heaven (with all of God's spiritual dimensions and mansions) also dwell within us. Believers are sealed in the cross.

Personal Reflection Moment

1. Are you a Christian?
2. Does your life exhibit the Fruits of the Spirit?
3. Have you ever checked up on yourself to see if you have really been saved?

    The Word of God's faith is near you! But is it in your mouth and in your heart? If you confess with your mouth the Lord Jesus is the Christ and believe in your heart (imagination) that God raised Jesus from the dead, you will be saved. For the heart (imagination) believes unto righteousness, and with the mouth forming creative words, confession is made unto salvation (Romans 10:8-10).

4. Do you pass the test?
5. Do you feel Christ's love, wisdom, power and presence operating within you? You need concrete evidence of your salvation, not just subjective hearsay or speculations.
6. Have you considered the possibility that you are only pretending to be a Believer in name only but denying the power of Christ?

It is important to examine yourself to see whether you are solid in the faith, not taking salvation for granted. If your faith is in Christ and He is in you, then All Things are possible, for Christ is mighty toward you. Jesus said that every word would be established by the mouths of two or three witnesses. If the Word of truth and Jesus Christ reside within, you will be sure of His abiding presence, because you couldn't do otherwise.

Jesus Christ imagined the whole universe. He conceived, formed and created everything that exists. Nothing in the world exists that Christ did not make, He even fashioned you. The divine body of Christ living within us removes our limitations and celebrates our strengths, so that we are triumphant in His abiding presence. For though Christ was crucified in weakness, He lives by the power of God. For we are weak compared to Him, but we shall live with Him by the power of God toward you.

> *We are not to do evil, but remain honorable. Believers are complete in Christ, of good comfort, of one mind and body, living in peace because the God of peace dwells within us. So, because the grace of the Lord Jesus Christ, and the love of God, and the communion of the Holy Spirit in within us all, we can do nothing against the truth, but for the truth* (2 Corinthians 13:7–8).

We can imagine, believe, dream and see who we are in Christ when we recognize that the greatness of Christ is living within us. By doing this, we awaken the Christ that is within us to give Him a body through which to express Himself.

Jesus recognized that He must lay down His own life and return to His Father's glorious heavenly mansions in order to bring forth many firstborn sons and daughters in His image.

> *I must fall and die like a kernel of wheat that is buried into the furrowed ground of the earth's soil. Unless I willingly die, I will remain alone a solitary seed. But My death will bring forth many new wheat seeds, sprouts and reproduce Myself many times over in a plenteous harvest of new Believers. In the same way I must die to self, bring forth life, anyone who holds onto their carnal life as it is, will destroy their life. But, if we let go of our sinful life, receive Christ's salvation, becoming reckless in our love, we will have eternal life forever* (John 12:24–25).

The word of the Lord came to Abram in a vision, "Do not be afraid, Abram. IAM your shield, your exceedingly great reward." But Abram replied, "Lord GOD, what will You give me, seeing I go childless, You have given me no offspring born to my house, and the heir of my estate is Eliezer of Damascus?" The word of the Lord responded, "This Eliezer shall not be your heir."

Abram fell into a deep sleep and beheld horror and great darkness. The Lord made a covenant with Abram saying, "To your descendants I have given this land, from the river of Egypt to the great River Euphrates, the Kenites, the Kenezzites, the Kadmoties, the Hittites, the Perizzites, the Raephiam, the Amorites, the Canaanites, the Girgashites and the Jubusites. Your descendants will be strangers in a land that is not their own, they will serve them for four hundred years. I will judge that nation and your descendants will come out with great possessions" (see Genesis 15:1–14).

The number 400 represents Abraham's promise of a son being fulfilled until the Exodus. The number 400 is the Hebrew letter *tav*, which means *a sign of the Eternal King's truth dealing with the past, present and future things in the material world, life or death.*

5 (grace) x 8 (Christ) x 10 (in full) = 400

40 (testing) x 10 (done) = 400

8 (Jesus) x 50 (Jubilee) = 400

Tav is the twenty-second letter in the Hebrew alphabet. It represents a mark.

As Believers, we awaken the Christ in us to become spiritual beings. We are sealed with an invisible cross that we wear on our body. After a lifetime of testing, man's final destination is determined. We gladly pick up and proudly wear our cross (this body of flesh) daily. In life, we must all bear our own cross. The four hundred years represents the bearing of the sign of the cross in our physical bodies, while our spirit man longs to be with, please and follow God.

The Spirit of the Lord is sent by the Father to draw, lead, guide and levitate us in-between heaven and earth, and He is sent to carry and transport us geographically or translate us into the heavenly realms. *So the Spirit lifted me up and took me away, and I went in bitterness, in the heat of my spirit; but the hand of the Lord was strong upon me* (Ezekiel 3:14).

The hand of the Lord carries us into the Spirit. Then through a dream, word of knowledge or the Spirit of Wisdom or Counsel, we are enlightened by a vision to know God's will and desire for our life.

> *He stretched out the form of a hand and took me by a lock of my hair; and the Spirit lifted me up between earth and heaven, and brought me in visions of God to Jerusalem, to the door of the north gate of the inner court, where the seat of the image of jealousy was, which provokes to jealousy* (Ezekiel 8:3).

We are taken up by the Spirit of the Lord into a specific realm of the Spirit to see vision. When vision is granted, we can pray in agreement with God's perfect plans and purposes for our life, for our family and friends and for the cities, states or nations of the world. By asking in accordance to God's divine nature and perfect will, Jesus continues to come to us with the provision of the exact key, wisdom, knowledge, anointing, glory realm or weapon we need.

> *And that's not all. You will have complete and free access to God's Kingdom. I have given you the keys of the kingdom of heaven to open any and every door: no more barriers between the kingdom of heaven and earth, earth and heaven. A yes on earth is yes in heaven. A no on earth is no in heaven. Whatever you bind and declare to be improper and unlawful on earth must be what is already bound in heaven; and whatever you loose and declare lawful on earth must be what is already loosed in heaven* (Matthew 16:19).

When by faith we receive the comings of Jesus, He will share with us the secret knowledge that has been placed in reserve for us in that particular mansion. God's wisdom grants us admittance to heaven's hidden treasures. These spiritual rooms of wealth store all the vast resources of heaven that give us the ability to formulate the exact strategy to overcome any and all weapons formed against us on any level or in any parallel realm.

Jesus has gone before us to prepare a place of abundance for us in the Father's spiritual house.

Believers have been given the keys to defeat death, hell and the grave. We defeat our last enemy (death) by learning how to use the keys of the Kingdom of God effectively. The beloved John, the revelator, was imprisoned, but he could not be restrained from receiving the keys. In Revelation 1:9–20, John could not be stopped from hearing a voice behind him, from having a vision or from entering into the realm of the Spirit through prayer.

> *I, John, with you all the way in the trial and the kingdom and the passion of patience in Jesus, was banished, imprisoned on the island called Patmos because of God's Word, the witness of Jesus. It was Sunday and I was in the Spirit, praying.* (Note that it is evident John had already stepped into other dimensions prior, because the voice he heard was behind him.) *I heard a loud voice behind me, trumpet clear and piercing: "Write what you see into a book. Send it to the seven churches: Ephesus, Smyrna, Pergamum, Thyatira, Sardis, Philadelphia, Laodicea." I turned and saw the voice.*

Have you ever seen a voice? Are you able to see into the invisible realm of the Spirit? Spiritual sight of color and sound are some of the keys we must learn how to use. When we, like John, enter into this particular realm of the Spirit, we will see things, be able to record what was seen and then speak of things we have never seen and do things we have never done before. This is how the Sons of God will arise to shift the kingdoms of this world. If we are not able to hear, see, feel or perceive in the realm of the Spirit, we are not able to receive anything from the Spirit.

If we are not able to hear, see, feel or perceive in the realm of the Spirit, we are not able to receive anything from the Spirit.

> *I saw a gold menorah with seven branches, and in the center, the Son of Man in a robe and gold breastplate, hair a blizzard of white, eyes pouring fire-blaze, both feet furnace-fired bronze, the force of His voice was a cascading torrent, right hand holding the seven stars, His mouth a sharp-biting sword, His brilliant face shone as the brightest sun. I saw this and fainted dead at His feet. His right hand pulled me upright, His voice reassured me: "Don't fear: IAM First, IAM Last, IAM Alive. I died, but I came to life, and My life is now forever. IAM the God who is, the God who was and the sovereign-strong God who is about to arrive on the scene. See these keys in My hand? They open and lock death's doors, they open and lock hell's gates. Now write down everything you see:*

> *things that are, things about to be. The seven stars you saw in My right hand and the seven-branched gold menorah—do you want to know what's behind them? The seven stars are the angels of the seven churches; the menorah's seven branches are the seven churches."*

We are granted the ability to rest in God's peace and apprehend His blessings. We are then admonished to flow into that greater realm of glory. *Now may the God of peace Himself sanctify you completely; and may your whole spirit, soul, and body be preserved blameless at the coming of our Lord Jesus Christ* (1 Thessalonians 5:23).

Spiritual knowledge and understanding give us an increased ability to imagine on a much larger scale. When we are redeemed in Christ, we become a new creature with supernatural abilities. We quickly learn how to open the doors to new mansions, enter into diverse dimensions and explore that part of the Kingdom of God or heavenly places that are only found in Christ. *Blessed be the God and Father of our Lord Jesus Christ, who has blessed us with every spiritual blessing in the heavenly places in Christ* (Ephesians 1:3).

Hidden Doors

It is important to include here that just as there are hidden doors within homes, buildings and other structures in the natural realm, there are also mystical doors of access hidden in the sacred, transcendent realms of the invisible. One biblical example of a door of access being hidden is found in the account of Lot hosting the angelic messengers in his home. The men of the town wanted to lay with the angels who were staying in Lot's home. Lot stepped out of his home to try and reason with the men of his community. The Bible records that the riotous gang of excited men would have nothing to do with Lot's request to respect his house guests.

> *They all came rushing at Lot yelling, "Stand back!" They aggressively pressed Lot hard against the door until it bowed and was about to break. They sneered amongst themselves, "This man Lot came to stay here amongst us temporarily, and now he presumes to act like our judge. We will deal more severely with you than with these two men if you do not turn them over for our enjoyment."*

> *The crowd of lustful men pressed their bodies against Lot's until the door was about to break open into his house. But, just at the breaking point, the angels inside of Lot's house reached out and pulled Lot into his home with them, shutting the door securely behind him to block the Sodomites out. The heavenly messengers struck all of the angered men with blindness who were pressing the door both young and old, great and small alike. It wasn't long before the whole mob had exhausted themselves, wearily groping for the door frame in their darkness and blindly grasping for a door that was in plain sight just seconds before* (Genesis 19:9–11).

When the angels shut off the access to Lot's natural, earthly door, the violent men's eyes were blinded, preventing them from gaining access to the very present door that gave entrance into Lot's home. The angels protected Lot, his entire family and themselves from being invaded by abusers who meant them harm.

There are positive, angelic creatures of light and negative, demonic beings of darkness that have a supernatural ability to blind our eyes from spiritual and natural doors of access. Often a blessing is hiding right in front of our face; for certain the answer is right under our nose. As we learn to speak what God sends, we will be granted permission to proceed and ascend into a higher realm of favor. But without imagining what could be, praying and seeking to find the dimensional doors, we remain sterilely held in poverty, limited to one dimension.

> Spiritual knowledge and understanding give us an increased ability to imagine on a much larger scale.

As you consider these mysteries revealed, bear in mind that God takes great pleasure in us using our sanctified imagination to seek and to find. God has not placed any restrictions on us. The Spirit of the Lord has liberated us from the earthly realm. God desires for us to prosper and increase as our soul prospers. *Now the Lord is the Spirit; and where the Spirit of the Lord is, there is liberty* (2 Corinthians 3:17). Once we access a new, higher level of being, it is necessary to sustain (rest in) our state of being in God.

CHAPTER SIX

Spiritual Ascension

Everything in the Bible is a parabolic picture of how to access everything Christ has given us through our imagination. God combines different symbolic pictures, numbers and colors in various settings to communicate a grand story message to us in dreams and visions. God uses symbols because a picture is much easier to remember than a statement. A symbol will imprint on our spirit, so we can easily recall it. The symbolism God chooses to place together tells an amazing story that speaks a thousand different words to every individual.

From Genesis to Revelation, the Bible uses symbolism to represent Satan as a serpent, Draco the Dragon or Hydra. Jesus the Messiah is seen as the seed, the roaring, majestic Lion and the gentle, sacrificial Lamb who is slain. Christ Jesus goes forth to triumphantly conquer. Jesus is seen bruised, pierced and slain on the cross for the salvation of mankind.

The symbolism of the twelve constellations declares God's glory and is another illustration of His signs for man—so that we may see and know what He is doing. *God determines and counts the number of the stars; He calls them all by their names. Great is our Lord, mighty and of great power; His understanding is infinite, inexhaustible and boundless* (Psalm 147:4–5).

We learned previously that the number six represents man. Six doubled equals twelve, which represents God's divine government, order or rule. The number twelve also represents the spiritual realm, creativity and illumination and the elect purposes of God. I will begin with the twelve constellations, lead into the account of Jacob's transformational and spiritual ascension through the gateways God has provided and return to the significance of twelve.

The signs of the heavens are original star pictures developed by God; He calculated their precise movements. God created the stars for the telling of times, seasons and signs. The star constellations also tell the gospel beginning with Virgo (the Virgin Mary) and ending with Leo (the return of the Lion of Judah, Jesus). Have you ever looked up to gaze with wonder into a star-lit night to enjoy the pageantry of the millions of brilliant stars? Each star and its unique name tell a glorious gospel story for the whole world to know.

> *God created the stars for the telling of times, seasons and signs.*

God directed Abraham to use his imagination as he looked up at the stars. The Enteral One wanted Abraham to understand the greatness and magnitude of His promise to him. *Then He brought him* (Abraham) *outside and said, "Look now toward heaven, and count the stars if you are able to number them." And He said to him, "So shall your descendants be"* (Genesis 15:5).

The stars reveal the limitlessness of God. Because we are co-heirs with Christ, we have access to that very limitlessness of God. When you look up at the constellations, do you see God's promises and purposes revealed? Do you hear the stars' frequencies singing the beauty of His glory? The heavens declare the glory of God; the firmament shows and proclaims His handiwork.

> *Day after day pours forth speech, and night after night knowledge is shown forth and revealed. There is no speech, language nor spoken word from the stars; where their voice is not heard. Yet their voice in evidence goes out through all the earth, the words of their sayings to the end of the world. Of the heavens has God made a tent for the sun* (Psalm 19:1–4).

Tragically, carnal man has redirected his focus on the created stars and planets and on their alignment (horoscopes), instead of looking to the Creator, for knowledge and wisdom. My intention of including the following material on the constellations is to highlight and explain the mighty works and mysteries of God.

The Twelve Constellations

All-knowing God granted the Antediluvian people such a long life that they were able to perfect the 600 year-long star cycle in astronomy. This celestial cycle was known as a Grand or Great Year! Once a person had lived 600 years, each additional year furnished even more proof of the heavenly star cycle's accuracy. The Antediluvians knew the original meanings of each of the stars contained in the twelve constellations, and they knew how they all related together. We know Enoch walked with God and is reported to have visited heaven on many occasions. Enoch prophesied God's final victory through the stars.

> *Then God said, "Lights come out! Let there be lights in the sky's and firmament of the heavens to divide the day from the night; and let them be for signs and mark seasons, and for days and years; and let them be for lights in the firmament of the heavens to give light on the earth;" and there it was so. Then God made two great lights: the greater light to rule the day, and the lesser light to be in charge of the night. He made the stars also. God set them in the firmament of the heavens to give light on the earth, and to rule over the day and oversee the night, and to divide the light from the darkness. And God saw that it was good. So, the evening and the morning were the fourth day* (Genesis 1:14–19).

There were twelve brothers, each one corresponding with a particular one of the Twelve Tribes of Israel. Each tribe was assigned to one of the twelve constellations (zodiac means *animal circle*). *After this, Jacob called all of his twelve sons to him. "Gather near to me, so I can let you know what to expect in the days to come. Gather around and pay attention, you sons of Jacob. Listen carefully, my sons, to Israel, your father"* (Genesis 49:1–2).

All these are the unique tribes of Israel, the twelve (journey paths of) *tribes: and this is what their father said to them as he blessed them, blessing* (to draw down to) *each one with his own special, farewell blessing* (Genesis 49:28).

The following are the names of the children who were born to Jacob by his wives and concubines (Leah birthed Reuben, Simeon, Levi, Judah, Issachar and Zebulum. Zilpah birthed Gad and Asher. Bilhah birthed Dan and Naphtali. Rachel, Jacob's favorite wife, birthed Joseph and Benjamin, his two favorite sons.):

- *Reuben* (Aquarius)—life-giving energy of the first man; unstable like water; some consider him to be Taurus the Bull.
- *Simeon* (Capricorn)—the sacrifice; aggressive, furious anger.
- *Levi* (Pisces)—attached, joined to the divine; to serve a higher call; some consider him (and Simeon) to be the twin Gemini.
- *Judah* (Leo)—praise; acknowledgement; of a selfless path; of a leader.
- *Issachar* (Cancer)—he will bring a reward; scholarly wisdom; clarity of direction.
- *Zebulun* (Aries)—the marketplace business person.
- *Gad* (Sagittarius)—fortune; warrior ready to fight for his values and beliefs in justice; to protect freedom.
- *Asher* (Libra)—abundant prosperity; enjoys pleasure.
- *Dan* (Scorpio)—judge; justice; law and order.
- *Naphtali* (Virgo)—free, independent spirit; to struggle the birth or to wrestle; to break out of mediocracy.
- *Joseph* (Taurus)—thrives through suffering; overcomes all adversaries; maintains spiritual integrity; uses his imagination to interpret dreams and achieve greatness.
- *Benjamin* (Gemini)—hungry for the divine.

Children born to Joseph and his wife Asenath were *Manasseh* (remains connected to his spiritual roots) and *Ephraim* (fruitful in the land of affliction).

It is very difficult to assign one specific constellation to each tribe, as we are only sure of the four standards represented in the faces of the four living creatures.

> *Can you bind together a cluster of twinkling stars—or catch*

> *the eye of the seven beautiful sisters of Pleiades who keep company in the night sky? Can you loosen the cords of Orion's bow? Or distract him from his hunt? Can you lead the stars of the zodiac out in their proper seasons, get Venus to look your way, and guide the Great Bear with her cubs to come out and play? Do you know the rules of the heavens, or the first thing about the sky's constellations, how they affect things on Earth or apportion their influence on the seasons* (Job 38:31–33)*?*

In His great wisdom, God gave us the heavenly stars, the moon and the sun for signs and seasons and to help us keep time. Each zodiac has three constellations, which makes a total of thirty-six. With the twelve signs, we come to a total of forty-eight: 36 + 12 = 48 (4 x 12). A complete circle in heaven is 360 degrees, which consists of 12 x 30.

In the Bible, Numbers 2 reveals the layout of Israel's camp that was revealed to Moses long after Jacob bestowed his blessing to his sons (after he described the twelve as the animals of the zodiac in Genesis 49). The original identification of the tribes with the twelve constellations must have preceded Jacob's blessings, as indicated by Joseph's dream that the constellations bowed down to him in Genesis 37:9. Jacob's blessings were, therefore, a revolutionary prophetic word that was necessitated by the revealed characters of the brothers. The underlying layout of the camp of Israel can be reimagined by comparing it to the blessings of Genesis 49 and Deuteronomy 33.

God is directing each and every one of us to go beyond into the certain place of encounter so that we can obtain more of Jesus.

The four faces of the cherubim are represented by the Lion, Man, Ox and Eagle:

- *East* (Lion)—Judah, Issachar, Zebulon
- *South* (Man)—Reuben, Simeon, Gad
- *West* (Ox)—Ephraim, Manasseh, Benjamin
- *North* (Eagle)—Dan, Asher, Naphtali

The twelve constellations of the Mazzaroth and Hebrew Calendar:

- *Aries*—Nisan (March and April)
- *Taurus*—Iyar (April and May)
- *Gemini*—Sivan (May and June)
- *Cancer*—Tammuz (June and July)
- *Leo*—Av (July and August)
- *Virgo*—Elul (August and September)
- *Libra*—Tishrei (September and October)
- *Scorpio*—Cheshban (October and November)
- *Sagittarius*—Kislev (November and December)
- *Capricorn*—Tevet (December and January)
- *Aquarius*—Shevat (January and February)
- *Pisces*—Adar (February and March)

A Supplanter's Journey

After Jacob deceived Isaac, so he could take Esau's blessing, he supplanted Esau as the firstborn son. Because of Esau's rage, Jacob was driven into exile. He was chased from all of his newly-gained blessings, his beloved mother and father, his friends and all of his inheritance. He was forced into a wilderness journey where his now foe, Esau, was an expert navigator. Jacob had to run from everything and everyone he was familiar with. Although Jacob was alone, God was with him. *Then you will know which way to go, since you have never been this way before* (Joshua 3:4).

The promises of God are on the move, opening up spiritual and territorial gateways so that we can access celestial doors.

The true God who inhabits sacred space is a Father to the fatherless. He adopts sons and places the solitary in families. He is a defender of widows. He makes a home for those who are alone. He frees the prisoners and leads them to prosper. Yet those who rebel against Him live in the barren land without His blessings and prosperity (see Psalm 68:5–6).

At the age of seventy-six (means *prophet*), Jacob didn't have anyone to depend on in a hostile territory, except God. He was left all by himself in an unknown land. At least Isaac had had Eleazar to bridge the Rebecca gap. Jacob was running away from his past while trying to find his future home, some semblance of security and the support of a family. God had begun a good work in Jacob, and He had promised to finish it. Jacob was learning how to take steps of faith, to acknowledge God in all of his ways and in all places. And God directed his paths. *In all thy ways acknowledge Him, and He shall direct thy paths* (Proverbs 3:6).

This is the account of Jacob, the supplanter (see Genesis 28:10–22):

> Jacob left Beersheba and traveled toward Haran (a dry, parched land). Jacob's dream of home had turned into a nightmare, as he had to run for his life into a barren, dark, uncertain place. Jacob was fleeing into the hands of Laban (white), the master deceiver. As dusk approached one day and the sun dipped its head to sleep, Jacob came to a 'paga' *certain place of destiny* where he could stay for the night.
>
> This was Jacob's divine appointment—where he collided with the certainty of God's blessing of destiny, and a new, God-directed day of abundance dawned. This certain place recognized Jacob the minute he stepped onto that sacred ground; Abraham had already offered a sacrifice of prayer in that place for him.
>
> *For I have chosen Abraham so that he will direct his children and his household after him to keep the way of the Lord by doing what is right and just, so that the Lord will bring about for Abraham what He has promised him* (Genesis 18:19).
>
> Across the desert horizon, Jacob saw the ancient stones scattered that generations before his forefather, Abraham, had used to build a prayer altar.
>
> *Abraham was now very old, and the Lord had blessed him in every way* (Genesis 24:1).
>
> Jacob chose and carefully arranged some smaller stones under his head for support as he lay down to sleep. I will fear

> no terror by night; I will have faith, not fear. Jacob prayed, "God, I ask that you open the starry heavens and reveal my future in this sacred place of prayer." During the night, God gave Jacob a dream.
>
> *Yet the Lord will command His loving-kindness in the daytime, and in the night His song shall be with me, a prayer to the God of my life* (Psalm 42:8).
>
> In the dream, Jacob saw a magnificent, helix-shaped ladder set up on the earth; its top reached to the heavens. Jacob saw some beautiful angelic messengers from his past ascending and a totally new envoy of angels descending into his future, ascending and descending on this spiral staircase. At the very top stood the Lord, the Eternal One.
>
> The speaking Spirit said, "IAM the Lord, the Eternal One! IAM the God of Abraham, your forefather, and the God of your father, Isaac. The land on which you are now lying is the land I have promised to give to you and your descendants. Your descendants will be as many as there are specks of dust on the earth. You will spread out to the west, east, north, and south. Through your descendants, all the families of the earth will find true blessing. Know IAM with you, and I will watch over you no matter where you go. One day I will bring you full circle back to this land. I will not leave you or forsake you until I have done all I have spoken and promised you."
>
> The dream ended, and Jacob woke up from his sleep. Jacob was obviously shaken when he fearfully spoke to himself, "There is no doubt in my mind that the Eternal One is in this place—and I didn't even know it! This 'paga' certain place of destiny is absolutely awesome! It can be none other than the house of God and the gateway into heaven!"

God is directing each and every one of us to go beyond into the *certain place* of encounter so that we can obtain more of Jesus. Jesus created, oversees and, at the right time, selects every dream that is within us. At every crossroad and strategic time in our life, Jesus descends heaven's ladder, just like He did for Jacob, to enter our dreams and enhance our imagination. He descends to touch us, to enter our mind's eye and to awaken us to places beyond our current belief. He ascends to stand watch over our dreams and broaden our imagination at the top of heaven's ladder. Christ beckons us to go beyond the known as we rest in His presence.

Beyond: Is a Place

Address only known by you
A place known by glimpses
Stolen during brief intervals
Of mind diverted reverie
Between dogged determination and
And dreamy imagination,
A projection into a land
Of peaceful, safe tranquility!

Keat Wade 04/23/19 (18 Nissan 5779)

> Jacob rose very early the next morning. Jacob took the altar stone he had placed under his head, set it up as a pillar and then poured oil on top of it to commemorate his experience with the Eternal One. He named that place Bethel, which means *house of God.* Before that, the name of the city had been called Luz. Then Jacob made a vow.
>
> Jacob declared, "Since God is going to be with me, keeping me safe on this journey and giving me bread to eat and clothing to wear so that I return to my father's house in peace, then the Eternal Lord will be my God. And this stone I have made into a pillar will be the first stone laid in God's house. And Lord, of everything You give me, I will give one-tenth always back to You."

Jacob was running from his past while trying to discover his true self. Jacob needed to learn to *rest* in God's presence in order to obtain the vision of his future purposes and destiny. Revelation brings enlargement, especially when our emotions are engaged to influence our thought processes as we relate to a God encounter.

On his journey, Jacob came to a *certain place* of destiny. He marked the place where his destiny was waiting for him with a rock. This certain place is the specific dwelling each individual must come to in their spiritual journey in order to awaken their imagination and connect with God. Jacob stayed in that precise place of visitation overnight. The sun had set on Jacob's past identity, for a new day of imagination was dawning on him.

You must be born again to see and enter the Kingdom of God, and it has been given to you to understand the mysteries of the Kingdom of God.

David knew the Rock. *Jesus is the Rock, His works are perfect, and all His ways are just. A faithful God who does no wrong, upright and just is He* (Deuteronomy 32:4). David described what Jacob was experiencing with the Rock, Jesus, in this way:

> *No matter where IAM, even when IAM far from home, resting at the end of the earth will I cry out to You for a Father's help. When IAM feeble, my heart is overwhelmed by life and IAM fainting; lead and guide me to the Rock that is higher than I, yes, guide me into Your glory to a Rock that is too high for me where IAM safe and sheltered* (Psalm 61:2).

Ruth followed Naomi as her rock stating, "Where you go, I will go."

The Rock followed Israel in the wilderness; there she could learn to rest by laying down her cognitive skills.

Our head has to enter into peace to find rest in the Holy Spirit. Rest empowers us to receive revelation knowledge so that we can obtain our destiny. Sleep empowers rest so that we can receive our instructions in the night season. Dreams empower us to live out our life in the dawn of a new day as we awaken in God's enlightenment.

God will open the heavens, drop a revelatory ladder down, send laterally-moving angelic messengers and do whatever it takes to get His destiny plans to us. God promises to give His beloveds sleep so that He can cause us to rest in a higher plane of heaven's glory. *When you lie down, you will not be afraid; yes, you will lie down and your sleep will be sweet* (Proverbs 3:24).

God is continually working on our behalf, even while we are sound asleep.

> *God does speak in one way and even another way—yet no one may be able to perceive what He says. One kind of answer God gives comes in the form of a dream—in a night-vision—when deep slumber comes to people who have lain down to sleep in their beds. Yes, this is often when He opens the ears of humanity, and seals their life-corrections in the terrors of the night so that He can turn one away from his evil deeds and put down the arrogance of the proud. He does all of this so that He might hold back one soul from the pit and protect one life from passing over to the land of death* (Job 33:14–18).

God is working All Things according to the counsel of His will for those who love Him, so they can obtain an inheritance in Him.

> *In Him we also were made to be God's heritage portion and we also obtained an inheritance; for we had been foreordained, chosen by God and appointed beforehand in accordance with His purpose, Who works out everything in agreement with the counsel and design of His own perfect will* (Ephesians 1:11).

Spiritual Gateways

Because Jacob's imagination was awakened, he dreamed of a ladder that reached from earth to heaven. The angels of God ascended (Jacob's old thoughts, ways and ideas of a past season went up) and descended (a new season of God's grand thoughts, imaginative ideas and ways) on the ladder, flooding into Jacob a new reality! The Lord simultaneously stood over Jacob at the top of the heavenly ladder and rested within Jacob's mind as he slept on the earth. The Lord was bilocated as a connecting ladder that descended from heaven to join Himself with man on earth (see John 1:51).

Jacob arranged the stones at the head place where he had lain down. In his dream, the angels of God also ascended and descended on Jacob; the Son of Man brought him revelation knowledge and spiritual insights about his calling and destiny. In this certain place of destiny, Jacob had a collision with the favor of God. Heaven's door was open to Jacob! It is also open to you and me.

Jesus was demonstrating to Jacob how to gain access to one of heaven's open gateways.

> *After this I looked, and behold, a door standing open in heaven! And the first voice which I had heard addressing me like the calling of a war trumpet said, "Come up here* (progressing in an upward movement in the Spirit, from faith to anointing, to enter the glory realms), *and I will show you what must take place in the future"* (Revelation 4:1).

The promises of God are on the move, opening up spiritual and territorial gateways so that we can access celestial doors. The Word of God is sent forth to accomplish the will and purposes of God with His divine power. Christ is the wisdom and power that is resident within our imagination. These ancient gates are connected by spiritual ladders that rest upon the earth. They are revelatory highways that serve as spiritual lifelines to funnel the divine knowledge of God into our dreams of the night. They act like umbilical cords that feed us with heavenly knowledge and understanding so that we can be nurtured to grow and mature as God's spiritual inheritance here on earth.

We will find what we are looking for in Christ if we sift through the clamor of everything around us to seek for wisdom like some precious prize of silver, to search for godly wisdom skillfully like a hidden or buried treasure (see Proverbs 2:4). God works on our behalf in the hidden, dark places of night vision. Hidden treasures are discovered in darkness. *I will give you hidden treasures and wealth tucked away in secret places; I will reveal them to you. Then you will know that IAM the Eternal, the God of Israel, who calls you by name* (Isaiah 45:3).

> *Man is able to access these spiritual gateways through his imagination and through prayer, dreams and visions while he is on earth.*

Adam was put to sleep so God could open him up (exposing some of his hidden gifts) and build Eve (a perfect helper) out of his inner being.

It pleased God to reveal His Son to Saul on the road to Damascus. Later on, God revealed His presence in and through Paul.

> *I have been crucified with Christ in Him I have shared His crucifixion; it is no longer I who live, but Christ the Messiah lives in me (as my imagination); and the life I now live in the body I live by faith in by adherence to and reliance on and complete trust in the Son of God, Who loved me and gave Himself up for me* (Galatians 2:20).

It is no longer I who live. It is Christ who lives in and through me. So that we might become the righteousness of God in Him, Jesus freely gave Himself for us. He is not hiding from us. He is living resident within us. There is new vision He wants to give us so we do not perish. David said, *As for me, I will continue beholding Your face in righteousness* (rightness, justice and right standing with You); *I shall be fully satisfied, when I awake to find myself beholding Your form and having sweet communion with You* (Psalm 17:15).

Each of us must become our best, unique self who is comfortable in our own skin with no false pretense. We must continually abide in God's presence to reflect His glorious image. *I call to remembrance my song in the night; with my heart I meditate and my spirit searches diligently* (Psalm 77:6).

There is an evening and a morning when we reach the end of our natural resources or abilities, and we lie down in our place, trusting God and having the faith to enter into kingdom dominion. You must be born again to *see* and *enter* the Kingdom of God, and it has been given to you to *understand* the mysteries of the Kingdom of God.

John 13 depicts the story of Jesus taking off His outer robe, exposing His nakedness, and covering His secret or private parts with a towel. To demonstrate His love, Jesus bent down to wash each of His disciples' feet. Each time Jesus washed a pair of feet, He removed the dust (confusion) and dirt (sin or worldly understanding) in order to reveal the Head of Creation. Jesus removed the towel from His loins to dry their feet. By doing so, He revealed the need for their spiritual circumcision by removing the veil of flesh.

It was God's faith that immersed us into Jesus, the Anointed One, so that we can prepare our hearts and minds for action, firmly fixing our hope in

His marvelous grace. Now that we are circumcised, we can be covered and clothed with *His* anointing and glory.

Faith focuses on things that are not present or hidden in order to bring them into existence. The power of faith moves hope forward to lay a firm foundation for the things that we desire to be built into our reality. It was by faith that previous generations were approved. Through faith, we understand that the universe was created and beautifully orchestrated by the power of God's spoken Word. He decreed, and the invisible realm gave birth to everything we now see. Everything was fashioned and birthed from that which is invisible (see Hebrews 11:1–3).

Our faith intentionally focuses our expectant agreement on receiving a greater measure of revelatory truth.

Jesus is the door and ladder we must ascend and descend to enter into heavenly places and mansions. To receive vision, we must be grounded in the truth of the gospel and the wisdom of God.

Lay down your thoughts and plans to enter into rest. Repetitively moving horizontally forward and backward between fear of failure and the success of an unknown future does not move us forward into prosperity; it digs a muddy rut of bondage that enslaves and buries. Do not focus on, reminisce or announce the negative experiences of the past. Instead, decide to decree and declare the bright, beautiful future. *Declaring the end and the result from the beginning, and from ancient times the things that are not yet done, saying, My counsel shall stand, and I will do all My pleasure and purpose* (Isaiah 46:10).

Man is able to access these spiritual gateways through his imagination and through prayer, dreams and visions while he is on earth. Imaginative prayer, dreams and visions will be expounded upon in subsequent volumes.

> *Lift up your head* (imagination), *O you* (twelve spiritual disciplines, senses; twelve tribes) *gates; and be lifted up, you ancient, age-abiding doors* (twelve constellations in heaven), *that the gospel story of the King of glory may be displayed and come in to rest in and be exhibited through you* (Psalm 24:7).

Again, these ancient doorways detailed in Scripture represent the twelve different constellations that constantly cycle throughout time to declare the gospel message and to announce the glory of the Lord from the heavens above. The twelve constellations of the heavens broadcast God's eternal plans and declare the glory of God. The gospel is prophesied in the starry groupings by their conjunctions and through the meanings of their names. Just as the twelve disciples' names also depict the twelve spiritual disciplines of the life of a mature Believer. I will expand on the twelve spiritual disciplines in Volume III.

Day after day, these ancient gates pour forth speech and lectures of wisdom, and night after night, they bring forth knowledge in the dreams and visions of our sleep. There is no speech, human voice or spoken word from the stars. Their voice is heard only in the pulsing sound frequencies and light waves that boldly sing out their harmonious message of life eternal. Yet their voice in evidence goes out through all the earth. Their sayings of truth fill the atmosphere to be spoken everywhere, even to the end of the world.

> *God has stretched out the heavens as a tent and made a massive dome for the sun, which is as a bridegroom* (Jesus, the Bright and Morning Star) *coming out of His honeymoon bedchamber. The starry hosts rejoice as a strong athletic man who is ready to run his course. The Word of God goes forth like a blanket of knowledge from one end to the far expanses of the endless realms of the heavens. God's celestial Word vaults across the skies from sunrise to sunset. It melts our snowcapped hearts or imagination and breaks up the dry, barren places in order to prepare the way for faith to enter our spirit and actively rest in our soul.*
>
> *Nothing and no one are hidden from the intense warmth of the Word. The law of the Lord is perfect. The revelation of God restores the whole person; the testimony of the Lord is sure, making wise the simple. The precepts of the Lord are right, His signs are clear and point out the right life path that will bring joy to the heart or creativity to the imagination. The commandments of the Lord are pure guidance. Their brightness enlightens the eyes with wisdom* (the twelve spiritual disci-

> plines) *necessary for one to make accurate detailed decisions. The reverent fear of the Lord is clean, enduring forever; the ordinances of the Lord are true and righteous altogether.*
>
> *The Word of God is nobler and more desirable than diamonds and emeralds set in pure gold. Their announcements and declarations are sweeter than spring-ripe strawberries* (represent the healing of the flesh) *and honey* (the sweet Word of God) *dripping from honeycombs. Moreover, God's Word warns His friends of danger; it reminds us of His faithfulness, illuminates our path, and gives us instructions to find hidden treasures. Without God who can find his way? Who can discern his lapses and errors? Forgive me, Lord. Cleanse me from my hidden and unconscious faults. Keep back Your servant also from presumptuous sins; let them not have dominion over me! Then shall I be blameless, and I shall be innocent and forgiven of my great transgression. As I pray each morning and night, let the words of my mouth create righteous imaginations for the meditation of my heart that are acceptable in Your sight, O Lord, my firm, impenetrable Rock and my Redeemer* (Psalm 19).

Spiritual ascension does not come to the vile or greedy. Favor eludes the self-centered, corrupt or malicious person. In order to ascend the virtuous rungs of heaven's vertical ladder and escape from being an earthbound, horizontal walker, we have to actively perceive, understand and accurately interpret spiritual signs. We must, ultimately, be doers of what was imagined by applying the wisdom and revelation we receive from the Holy Spirit into our waking lives.

By faith, we seek intimacy with the face of God. Our faith intentionally focuses our expectant agreement on receiving a greater measure of revelatory truth. Through the now movement of faith, we can obediently apply the living Word of God. By becoming an active doer of the Word, we make godly changes that renew our mind to think like the Christ who lives within. His mani-

All around us and within us, the Spirit of God is awakening our imagination to observe that creation is pregnant with birth pains.

fest presence enhances the levels of favor, power and influence that one can access and ascend to in his or her life.

Daily taking up our cross causes the development of our spiritual man. The things of the natural, carnal world pass away as we move from crawling like a caterpillar in the dust to rising like a beautifully-jeweled butterfly, freely ascending the cross to enter into the kingdom of the heavens. For we know that the whole creation has been moaning together as in the pains of childbirth until now.

All around us and within us, the Spirit of God is awakening our imagination to observe that creation is pregnant with birth pains. We, too, feel the pangs of birth. These sterile, barren bodies yearn for their full deliverance. Waiting on the Spirit of God does not diminish us any more than a pregnant mother waiting for nine months before she can deliver her baby. We are enlarged and stretched, growing up into our full capacity, until our time is accomplished to give birth.

> *Who have the first fruits of the Spirit, a joyful indication of the blessings to come, even we groan inwardly, as we wait eagerly for the sign of our adoption as sons—the redemption and transformation of our body at the resurrection. For in this hope we were saved by faith. But hope the object of which is seen is not hope. For who hopes for what he already sees? But if we hope for what we do not see, we wait eagerly for it with patience and composure. In the same way, the Spirit comes along side of us to help us be patient and helps us along with our birthing or transformation because of our weakness. We do not know what prayer to offer or how to offer it as we should, but the Spirit Himself knows our need and at the right time intercedes on our behalf turning our wordless sighs and aching groanings that are too deep for words into Spirit-filled prayers* (Romans 8:22–28).

Christ or our imagination knows us far better than we know ourself. Our Christ consciousness knows our subconscious' pregnant condition and keeps us present before God. That's why we can be so sure that every detail in our *love-for-God* life is worked into something good.

Christ said it this way, *If I be lifted up from the earth, I will draw all men unto*

Me (John 12:32). As followers of Christ's truth, our imaginative thoughts ascend. As we maintain our upward climb on the spiritual ladder, our ways also evolve in order to create our true identity. We are transformed from an embryo that has all the DNA markings of a butterfly held within its system into a brilliant creature of spiritual flight.

CHAPTER SEVEN

Transformation

The metamorphosis of a caterpillar is a transformational process that is necessary to permanently alter a crawling, earthbound caterpillar into a beautifully-winged butterfly of spiritual flight. The caterpillar undergoes drastic changes that revolutionize his whole being. Once the transformation process is complete, the butterfly struggles to free itself from its dark, isolated chamber. Once the death to the old is complete in us, we are resurrected into a new form of life so that true freedom and spiritual flight is acquired. The majestic butterfly emerges into a royal state of being with a much higher and imperial function.

During the caterpillar's metamorphosis, he is isolated but elevated to a higher position. He is left alone to hang between two strategic places or destinations where he chooses between two different natures. The caterpillar attaches his chrysalis to a branch; he is suspended in the air, dangling above the earth. In this place of spiritual suspension, he is shedding the limitations of the earthbound, carnal nature. However, he has not yet reached the spiritual nature of perfection. During his transition, he is limited, bound and locked inside a dark, narrow creative container. While the caterpillar is being restrained and pressurized, its inside organs are melting down. The caterpillar's guts literally liquidate and transform into a mass of cellular fluid called *imaginal cells*.

These imaginal cells have a creative force that vibrates at a higher frequency, intelligence and consciousness than the cells of the (former) lowly caterpillar. The imaginal cells assemble together, rearrange and realign in order to take the caterpillar through an evolutionary, transformational process. These revolutionary changes empower the caterpillar to transfer from being a horizontal, earthbound, spineless creature, who is at the mercy of everything and everyone, to becoming a majestic, graceful being of elegant flight.

When the caterpillar awakens to his new existence, he is no longer his former self. He has been totally transformed and revitalized into a new, magnificent image that is a contemporary, modernistic, state-of-the-art structural design that flutters and flies. He is full of light and has reflective colors. Beautiful, fragrant flowers bursting with sweet nectar surround the emergent butterfly. He learns to fly from flower to flower, ascending and descending on the open petals to drink deep and retrieve his sweet, honeyed rewards. His delicate wings give him flight, lifting him into the unlimited spaces of the heavenly realms.

> *We, the same as the butterfly, are called by God's grace to shed the old man and take on the image and likeness of Christ Jesus.*

Locked within the DNA of his being, the little caterpillar always had the potential to fly, yet his amazing abilities were hidden. His greatness was disguised, unrecognizable and buried deep within. It took a time of dying to his old self-image in order for him to transition and resurrect into his ultimate calling and higher state of being.

We, the same as the butterfly, are called by God's grace to shed the old man and go through a transformation process to take on the image and likeness of Christ Jesus. We fall as a seed buried in the depths of the dark ground to die alone. From death, the new man resurrects into a higher spiritual form of life that is imprinted with the image, the fragrance of wisdom and the power of Christ. The hope of obtaining glory causes us to mount up with the beautiful, multicolored wings of a butterfly. These are our first fluttering wings.

As a mother hen, we ache to gather, embrace, comfort and disciple spiritual children under our protective wings. Those who learn to continually wait upon the Lord get new strength. They learn how to spread their strong, majestic wings to catch the upward drafts of wind to soar like eagles. They run without growing tired, and they walk in the fullness of God's power.

As we continue to mature, we learn how to transport to different geographic regions. We ascend to soar with the wings of the Spirit of the Lord to translate into heavenly places. Whether we soar on the wings of an eagle or with the Spirit of the Lord, we are called to mount up with wings and catch the wind of the Spirit to ascend *Jacob's Ladder*. We are to take our place centered in Christ in order to be seated in heavenly places. When we discern a new gift that is resident within us, we are able to ascend by climbing up one more rung of the ladder through self-discovery.

The transformation process from a natural, earthly image to a heavenly image and likeness comes when we advance from one level of revelation knowledge to another higher realm of wisdom and understanding. God gives us the wisdom that is needed to see a greater purpose and to imagine a new vision so that we can secure our prosperous future. Once we agree with God's higher call for us to take wings, the heavenly vision is established in the heart of our earthen vessel. For the invisible desires of our heart to become real, they must be believed, seen in our imagination, affirmed as true by our spirit, focused on and then prayed into existence. *The secret things belong to the Lord our God, but those things which are revealed belong to us and to our children forever, that we may do all the words of this law* (Deuteronomy 29:29).

The transformation process from a natural, earthly image to a heavenly image and likeness comes when we advance from one level of revelation knowledge to another higher realm of wisdom and understanding.

When we take on the belief that we have already attained our new desire, achieved the next goal or entered into a higher state of being that we consistently manifest, we are able to actively demonstrate the kingdom of heaven on earth. *Clearly you are an epistle of Christ, ministered by us, written not with ink but by the Spirit of the living God, not on tablets of stone but on the tablets of flesh, that is, of the* (imagination) *heart* (2 Corinthians 3:3).

During transitional seasons, we learn how to regain all that the past has stolen from us. The restoration process is essential for our complete healing. God's restitution empowers us to gain the wisdom that is needed to both resolve and forgive past issues. We learn how to amend and remove offenses. We obtain God's grace to release the pain of abuse, trauma and bitterness. We apply Jesus' cleansing blood to wash away our regrets in order to heal our moral conscience.

Wholeness comes when our spiritual awareness recognizes that we have stepped into an enlarged place. Now we are clothed in God's radiant light that causes us to live in a new day of compensation and unlimited favor. God intends for us to inherit all of His heavenly assets as joint heirs in Christ. *And if children, then heirs—heirs of God and joint heirs with Christ, if indeed we suffer with Him, that we may also be glorified together* (Romans 8:17).

A new, Christ-centered identity will reveal different strategies that enable us to become giants whose stature crushes and defeats all of our opposition. We will vigilantly protect our borders while we continue to fight the enemy by advancing and conquering broader territories to continually expand the Kingdom of God.

When we choose to die to our self-absorbed state of being, we agree to change our current beliefs. By elevating the principles of our faith, we welcome the Holy Spirit's embrace. The increased presence of the Holy Spirit in our life improves our character, amplifies the measure of favor we have and (He) enhances our right standing.

When we adopt godly views and align our attitudes with the greatness of Christ the King, His presence raises our expectations. His wisdom and beauty surface to the forefront to shine in and through our countenance.

> *Lord, because of Your strength, the king is strong. Look how he rejoices in You! He bursts out with a joyful song because of Your victory! For You have given him his heart's desire, anything he has imagined and everything he asks for. You haven't withheld a thing from Your betrothed one. Rich blessings overflow with every encounter with You, and You placed a royal crown of gold upon his head. He wanted resurrection—You have given it to him and more! The days of his blessing stretch on one after another, forever! You have honored him and made him famous. Glory garments are upon him, and You surround him with splendor and majesty. Your victory heaps blessing after blessing upon him. What joy and bliss he tastes, rejoicing before Your face! For the king trusts endlessly in You, and he*

will never stumble, never fall. Your forever-love never fails and holds him firm (Psalm 21:1–7).

Before Jesus was crucified, He gathered His disciples in the Garden of Gethsemane and spoke, *I will no longer talk much with you, for the ruler of this world is coming, and he has nothing in Me* (John 14:30). Jesus was perfect in every way, spotless and sinless. He never did anything ungodly or wrong; therefore, Satan could not touch Him without His Father's permission. Jesus needed to lay down His life on our behalf to fulfill the Father's will.

After Jesus' announcement, a riotous crowd armed with weapons and covered by the darkness of night came to the Garden searching for Jesus. The only light the captors carried or possessed was a man-made (temporary) lantern, a fading torch of fire (man's futile effort to spark true wisdom, enlightenment and knowledge).

When the crowd inquired of the whereabouts of Jesus, the IAM of God boldly answered, "Here IAM (the way, eternal life, deliverance, truth and salvation) you have found Me! Now release (My disciples), and let all these other man-made ways go." Such power was released from Jesus that the violent crowd fell back to the ground, slain in the power dwelling within His presence.

> *During transitional seasons, we learn how to regain all that the past has stolen from us.*

Fearing His master's fate, because of man's lack of understanding, Simon Peter (means *perfected spiritual hearing*) immediately drew his sword of faith and struck the high priest's servant, Malchus (means *diligent, teachable servant*), severing his right ear. *I will lead the blind by a road they do not know; by paths they have not known, I will guide them. I will turn the darkness before them into light* (Isaiah 42:16).

Without hesitation, Jesus reached down, picked up the bloody ear and placed it back on Malchus' head. The ear was healed, fully restored to health. The religious, deaf spirit was gone. Subsequently, Malchus' hearing came forth into a higher level of function. After the servant came in contact with Jesus' healing touch, he was able to hear wisdom and understand spiritual knowledge to receive the authentic truth about life.

People cannot be wise about something or someone they do not really know. *Incline your ear and hear the words of the wise, and apply your heart to imagine My knowledge* (Proverbs 22:17). The presence of Christ dwelling within us has transformed us into who we are today. In our pursuit of God, we discover His unending love and complete acceptance.

The Holy Spirit shares His knowledge and divine wisdom with us so that we can obtain a fuller understanding of His ways of truth. *Wisdom is the principal thing; therefore, get wisdom. And in all your getting, get understanding* (Proverbs 4:7).

As we have learned, God's wisdom is not of this world. We only discover godly wisdom as we learn how to transition to a higher realm of understanding, confidently journeying from the known into the unknown. We ascend by gradually expanding higher and deeper in the anointing until we are able to transcend into limitless realms of the glory. Clothed in the glory, we pass into a higher wisdom and ever-increasing realm of layered glory to the succeeding endless levels of glory.

> God's restoration empowers us to gain the wisdom that is needed to both resolve and forgive past issues.

On earth, we exist in a specific level of spiritual understanding that dwells beneath that of heaven. Jesus is from above; He exists beyond the earthly realms of understanding. Although Jesus is not of this world, He dwells in earthen vessels made of clay. Jesus dwells in the heart of man. We will die in our sin if we do not believe that Jesus is the IAM, the only begotten Son, sent by God (see John 8:23-24).

The Pishon River is one of the four rivers that arose out of the Garden of Eden. Pishon means *the extension of the mouth's influence is changing*. The Pishon River encircles the entire land of Havilah, a region known for its pure gold. The Hebrew name *Havilah* means *circle*; it can also mean *twist, dance or writhe*. The circular Hebrew letter *Pey* looks like an open mouth. The Hebrew number *80* represents the speech of the prophetic mouth.

In the Hebrew year 5780 (Roman calendar year of 2020), let your mouth speak the words that describe what you have seen (in visions and dreams) in the past ten years during the seer season of Ayin (the wellspring of the eye). Now and for the next ten prophetic years is the time to prophesy, decree, declare, say and pray what is and was revealed to you.

I have found that God does things in seven to ten years cycles. For ten years, we learned how to see and operate in the seer realm of dreams and visions. *"I am the seer," Samuel replied. "Go up ahead of me to the high place, for today you are to eat with me, and in the morning, I will send you on your way and will tell you all that is in your* (imagination) *heart"* (1 Samuel 9:19).

As for me, far be it from me that I should sin against the Lord by failing to pray for you. And I will teach you the way that is good and right (1 Samuel 12:23).

God showed His Bride things that would be taking place in the future. I believe that after visions are given, we learn how to create and develop them through our prophetic speech. Words go deep to mine the garden soil of our (imagination) heart, to bring forth the pure, golden words of the Spirit of God. We will learn how to speak forth God's wisdom and plans and prophesy, decree and declare the will of the Lord so that it comes into existence in order to further the Kingdom of God. *"For I know the thoughts and plans that I have for you," says the Lord, "thoughts and plans for welfare and peace and not for evil, to give you hope in your final outcome"* (Jeremiah 29:11).

The thoughts we imagine and the words we speak are incredibly powerful; they can redefine our life by either bringing forth life or bringing forth death (blessing or cursing). We are to be cheerful in our faith and rejoice with a glad heart that continually expresses happiness, no matter what our life circumstances may be presently. *We are to persevere in prayer all the time, giving thanks to God for everything for this is the will of God for us at the moment* (1 Thessalonians 5:16–18).

> *When we choose to die to our present, self-absorbed state of being, we agree to change our current beliefs..*

Spiritual Helpers

Praying with the tongues of our heavenly language will cause our spirit man to grow in anointing and power so that we can move in the strength of God's glory. Just as God walked and talked with Adam and Jesus in the Garden, He comes in the form of the Holy Spirit to dwell within the heart (garden) of the Believer. He also sends angels to show us the ways of God so that we may be transformed.

> *Then an angel showed me a river of the water of life clear as crystal flowing out of Christ the Lamb, from under the majestic Throne of God.* (The living Word of God springs up from out of a living reservoir that dwells within our being. It increases in power and strength until it flows out of the belly, just like heaven's life-giving river.) *On either side of the river was the Tree of Life bearing twelve kinds of fruit* (fruit is developed through spiritual disciplines), *yielding its fruit every month* (the earth rotates on its heavenly course through one of the twelve constellations each month)*; and the leaves of this tree are for the healing of the nations* (Revelation 22:1–2).

The Bride of Christ, the enlightened bondservants and friends of God who see His face and bear His names on their foreheads, will use these healing leaves to extinguish the curse of sin, disease and death.

The angels in God's Kingdom are made up of God's glorious light, wind, breath and fire. Angels come to attention when they hear the Word of God spoken in faith. Angels take action, going before us to level the mountains and push down the Jericho walls that loom ahead of us. Angels open conscious doors of opportunity and point out the avenues that we have not yet discovered. Angels sheer up a rearguard behind us, rise up valleys and forge a broad highway for us to run on.

> *The thoughts we imagine and the words we speak are incredibly powerful; they can redefine our life by either bringing forth life or bringing forth death (blessing or cursing).*

Angels control all of the entryways that grant us access to the revelatory heavenly realms of wisdom, knowledge, power and authority. Angels open and close spiritual gateways to prayer, praise, anointings, giftings and the glory realms in order to grant or deny us access. These spiritual gateways open, ascend, shift vertically (up, down) or stay closed depending upon the purity of our heart, level of love, spiritual understanding of God's ways and the degree of the revelation knowledge we possess. Angels bring knowledge to us based on the principles of God we understand.

The pneumatic light energy of angels is fluid like the blood of Jesus that cleanses our systems. The presence of angels washes over us like the flowing of living, clean internal water. To understand how we can become aware of the angelic realms, we should first acknowledge their existence to ascertain their presence. When we learn how angels function, we can begin to cooperate with them. The more we learn about these beautiful creatures, the easier it will be to properly utilize the benefits and power of all the different types of angels. Anyone who is interested in learning about angels should read my best-selling, comprehensive book *Angels in God's Kingdom*.

God's Holy Spirit is present and dwelling within us like an invading breath of eternal life that fills up our lungs and courses through our blood.

God's Holy Spirit is present and dwelling within us like an invading breath of eternal life that fills up our lungs and courses through our blood. His Spirit is like cleansing water that surrounds us, encompasses us and fills in every part of our being. It is the ever-expanding presence of Christ dwelling within us that gives us the hope of reaching the realms of glory.

> *But you are not in the flesh but in the Spirit, if indeed the Spirit of God dwells in you. Now if anyone does not have the Spirit of Christ, he is not His. And if Christ is in you, the body is dead because of sin, but the spirit is life because of righteousness. But if the Spirit of Him who raised Jesus from the dead dwells in you, He who raised Christ from the dead will also give life to your mortal bodies through His Spirit who dwells in you* (Romans 8:9–11).

CHAPTER EIGHT

Encountering Glory

The beautiful face of God's radiant countenance brings the shining light of His favor upon us. Aaron understood this concept when he laid hands on, prophesied to and prayed a blessing over his sons. *The Lord bless you and keep you; the Lord make the light of His beautiful face shine upon you, and be gracious to you; the Lord lift up His radiant countenance upon you, and give you peace* (Numbers 6:24–26).

One of the Church's main problems we wrestle with today is the same problem Israel had centuries ago. We are too familiar with a God who we have only read about in books or heard about from others. We hardly know Him, because we lack a personal, intimate relationship with Him. A healthy relationship takes a lot of quality time to develop. Most individuals do not develop an intimate, God-fearing relationship with Jesus.

People tend to relate to God through others' stories or experiences. Many do not read or study the Bible on their own. Instead, they blindly believe whatever they are taught or told by the preachers they hire to represent them before God. Few people invest the time and effort necessary to learn how to pray effective prayers that reach the heart of God. People look first to the prophet to hear God's voice for them, to tell them what to do or how to prosper.

Jesus met with Moses face-to-face. Moses was a friend to God. He learned how to raise his eyes to meet the loving glance of the Creator. *So, the Lord spoke to Moses face-to-face, as a man speaks to his friend. And he would return to the camp, but his servant Joshua the son of Nun, a young man, did not depart from the tabernacle* (Exodus 33:11).

Joshua represents the generation who has a passion to continually remain in God's presence. Once Moses met God at the burning bush, he was able to overcome his worldly indulgences and political rulings. He renounced the occult Egyptian training he received while living in the palace of Pharaoh, pursued God with all his heart and led Israel through the wilderness to their Promised Land.

If a man or woman does not learn how to stand alone on their own two feet against the ways of the world, he or she will never be a successful leader in the Kingdom of God. A leader has the ability to take people where they say they want to go. But a truly great leader shapes people so that they can go where they didn't even know where they needed to go to find success. A great leader is strong but not rude. He is gentle and kind but not weak. He is brave and bold but not intimidating. He is humble but not shy. He is proud of his accomplishments but not arrogant. He uses humor and compliments to motivate others.

We are too familiar with a God who we have only read about in books or heard about from others.

The more time we spend in the presence of God, like Joshua and Moses, the more success we will experience, because when we are in His presence, we are being transformed into His amazing image and likeness. Although a face-to-face encounter always is wonderful, we have it even better than Moses and Joshua did, because now Jesus constantly surrounds and makes intercession for us, and He lives, indwells and moves within the Believer. It is the countenance of Christ that shines in and through our face; it lights up our entire being as a pillar of fire filled with the power of Christ's radiant out-shining.

After his *burning bush* experience, Moses became an intimate friend of God. God gave Moses directions on how to draw the nation of Israel out of bondage. Moses delivered Israel from their Egyptian slavery mentality. The IAM that IAM God sent Moses (deliverer; delivered; to be drawn out of water) to lead Israel into the freedom of the Promised Land.

Now on the day that the tabernacle was raised up, the cloud covered the tabernacle, the tent of the Testimony; from evening until morning it was above the tabernacle like the appearance of fire. So, it was always: the cloud covered it by day, and the appearance of fire by night. Whenever the cloud was taken up from above the tabernacle, after that the children of Israel would journey; and in the place where the cloud settled, there the children of Israel would pitch their tents. At the command of the Lord the children of Israel would journey, and at the command of the Lord they would camp; as long as the cloud stayed above the tabernacle, they remained encamped. Whether it was two days, a month, or a year that the cloud remained above the tabernacle, the children of Israel would remain encamped and not journey; but when the cloud was taken up, they would journey. At the command of the Lord they remained encamped, and at the command of the Lord they journeyed; they kept the charge of the Lord, at the command of the Lord by the hand of Moses (Numbers 9:15–23).

And it came to pass when Moses entered the tabernacle that the pillar of cloud descended and stood at the door of the tabernacle, and the Lord talked with Moses. All the people saw the pillar of cloud standing at the tabernacle door, and all the people rose and worshiped, each man in his tent door (Exodus 33:9).

The tabernacle in these passages represents each one of our bodies individually and collectively as a community of Believers. Our body is a movable tent or habitation for God that is covered with hair and skin. Our body is a temple created by and for the indwelling, intermingling and covering presence of God. We use our body as a place to worship God. The Spirit of God dwells within us as the Great IAM. The Scriptures depict God, the Great IAM, as being concealed in watery clouds of vaporous mystery, revelation and truth.

> *Our body is a temple created by and for the indwelling, intermingling and covering presence of God.*

Kabod Glory

God's Kabod glory has come to those who have eyes to see. The weighty presence of God dwells within our (imagination) heart and continually surrounds and overlays us. As we expand our knowledge to become intimate with God, we discover the vast powers held in each of His numerous names, divine characteristics and holy attributes, so we continually experience more and more of His glories than we have ever discovered before.

The prophet Ezekiel described God's glory as a fire from his waist upward and as a fire from his waist downward. In other words, a minister who was totally consumed with the fire of God (see Ezekiel 1:27–28). Today, we are those glorious ministers of fire who are carrying the government of God on our shoulders. The glory appears as a cloud that covers by day and as a pillar of fire that illuminates our mind and body by night. These manifestations of the glory also authorized, endorsed, approved and executed the covenant between God and Father Abraham (see Genesis 15:17).

When God thinks a thought or declares or decrees anything, it instantly steps out of its holding place to manifest in the now as an already created substance.

Glory means that we possess a bright opinion, so glory is a shifting of our earthly opinions about God to obtain the substance and the enduring glory of God Himself. An understanding of God's glory moves us into a higher way of thinking, where we possess godly thoughts and apprehend His higher ways. In the glory, my thoughts are larger and my ways are higher. God enlarges my borders when I go up into one of the Father's mansions to appear before the Lord my God (see Exodus 34:24; Deuteronomy 12:20).

When God thinks a thought or declares or decrees anything, it instantly steps out of its holding place to manifest in the now as an already created substance. God created times and seasons to keep everything from manifesting all at once. God's thoughts toward us are positive, weighty and precious. They are so vast that they outnumber the grains of sand, so many that we cannot count the sum of them (see Psalm 139:17–18)! When God enlarges our capacity to hold more of His glory, we will not just talk about following the ways of God, but the Lord will write His commandments on the tablets of our heart (see Psalm 119:32).

God's thoughts (the Hebrew word is *machashabah*) are His imaginations, His creatively-designed tapestry and witty inventions toward us. God's thoughts and imaginations are His precious meditations of His abundant, unending love, and they are full of His majestic peace that passes all understanding. There is no evil or malice in His plans. God's goal is to give us His courage, knowledge and strength to reach an expected glorious end (see Jeremiah 29:11).

God is not slow in His answers or in His activity toward us, for He created everything at the Genesis. God is waiting on us to discover His ways of glory; we are not waiting on Him. God has already answered every prayer, healed every disease, conquered every enemy and removed every mountain. He is waiting on us to take up our authority, enter into the realm of weighty glory and speak spirit words to prophesy life and deliverance, to decree and make powerful declarations that His Kingdom has come and that His will is done on earth.

Faith does not come by searching out information about God or by memorizing the Scriptures about Jesus. We obtain eternal life by placing our faith in God and by developing an intimate, personal, loving relationship with Jesus Christ (see John 5:39). The glory of God is concealed within God's Word. As kings, we are to search out hidden matters in order to gain wisdom and divine knowledge (see Proverbs 25:2).

Kabod means *the abundant honor, weighty glory and out raying of the heavy, divine presence of God.* Honor is linked to glory. The king's scepter and his signet ring carry a kingly majesty that represents his power to rule in God's favor by exercising His great authority. Believers must develop an understanding of how to connect with the glory of God through prayer. We learn to sustain His glorious presence through a life of continual worship. When we enter into the glory of God, we are able to apprehend all of our needs that have been concealed in the riches of His glory (see Philippians 4:19).

We obtain eternal life by placing our faith in God and by developing an intimate, personal, loving relationship with Jesus Christ.

The more of the Word of God we believe and hold to as true, activating its power in our life, the more we are transformed into His glory. The more glory that we contain, the more the angelic hosts of heaven will be attracted to the light of our shining. It is the glory of God that causes a spiritual outshining from our beings.

The glory of God rests on the altar of our heart. As we pray, prophesy, decree and declare our worship to God (crying, "Holy!" unto the Lord), a sweet incense rises up. Angels attend to God's glory in heaven and in our earthen vessels. We are becoming a new, expanded and improved dwelling place for the Holy Spirit. The angels have come with spiritual seam rippers to loosen and remove the old mantles that have restricted us from emerging into our full potential.

An understanding of God's glory moves us into a higher way of thinking, where we possess godly thoughts and apprehend His higher ways..

When great glory rests in us, there is a continual expectation of reflecting God's greatness. Peter experienced the out raying of the Kabod glory of God's manifested weighty presence as he ministered healing and deliverance in the marketplace. The brilliant glory that shines out of us blinds the enemy, so he cannot know our personal identity to retaliate against us. As we lift our heads and open the five spiritual gateways, the King of Glory, strong and mighty, comes in. He is the Lord of Hosts, our mighty battle sword, shield and buckler (see Psalm 24:6–9).

Interestingly, the root Hebrew word for glory is liver. The liver is the internal organ that houses the core of our passion, emotions and measure of courage. The liver filters the toxins and poisons out of our body to give us a clean, pure body that insures a prosperous life. The kidneys are also known to be the seat that houses our emotions. We will experience a full range of emotions throughout life. To maintain the health of our body, we must rid ourself of all toxic, harmful emotions. The kidneys and liver house the joy of the Lord that gives us our strength (see Nehemiah 8:10).

We are the physical dwelling place of God. The invisible Spirit of God infills every cell and every organ of our body.

> *For ever since the creation of the world God's invisible nature and attributes, that is, His eternal power and divinity, have*

> *been made intelligible and clearly discernible in and through us and the handiworks of the things that have been made. So, people are without excuse or any defense or justification for rejecting such a great and glorious love* (Romans 1:20).

The fullness of God's presence in our body becomes the measure of God's inheritance that is found in us. The fullness of the earth and our earthen vessels are the Lord's. His ability to expand our boundaries causes us to prosper in a new way of fullness. When God touches one area of our life, everything changes and our borders increase! When we agree with God, we accelerate into multiplication.

Jesus is high and lifted up, so His glory fills and lifts us. The Holy Spirit resides in us as His temple. We experience a consuming, purifying fire that enables us to speak the words of God.

> *Jabez was more honorable than his brothers, and his mother named him Jabez saying, "Because I bore him with pain." Now Jabez called on the God of Israel, saying, "Oh, that You would bless me indeed and enlarge my border, and that Your hand might be with me, and that You would keep me from harm that it may not pain me!" And God granted him what he requested* (1 Chronicles 4:9–10).

God targets and removes our sin, pain and weakness to help us discover the hidden gifts, our untapped talents and the neglected aspects of our being in order to create an upgraded, new and powerful self-image that is centered in Christ. God has placed His hand to uncover, awaken, call on, tap into and highlight the untrained gifts that are resident, yet hidden, deep within us. God longs to empower the dormant ideas, breathe on our new gifts and ignite those talents that have been concealed and never discovered or used before that are in the depths of our being.

> *When we enter into the glory of God, we are able to apprehend all of our needs that have been concealed in the riches of His glory.*

Moses desired to see God's glory and to know the ways of God. The same passing glory that Moses experienced as he was hidden, covered by God's hand in the cleft of the rock, now lives within the body of the Believer (see Exodus 33:19). Moses' face shone with the fading glory of God (see 2 Corinthians 3:13). It is different for Believers today; we all live in front of God with an unveiled face. We continue to behold and reflect the glory of God's Word as a mirrored image.

We are constantly being transfigured into His very own likeness in ever-increasing splendor from one degree of glory to another (see 2 Corinthians 3:18). As we discover more of God's ways, we become a newly renovated and expanded dwelling place for Christ's presence. It is time to lengthen our curtains, stretch out and increase and expand our borders. It is time to remove the dead, religious, legalistic weights and exchange them for the creative, life-giving and weighty Kabod presence of God's glory.

The fullness of God's presence in our body becomes the measure of God's inheritance that is found in us.

Isaiah 54:

> *"Shout for joy, barren one, you who have borne no child; break forth into joyful shouting and cry aloud, you who have not travailed; for the sons of the desolate will be more numerous than the sons of the married woman," says the Lord. "Enlarge the place of your tent; stretch out the curtains of your dwellings, spare not; lengthen your cords and strengthen your pegs* (view your future)."

(Claim Ephesians 3: expanded length, depth, breadth, height, new dimension and paradigms.)

> *"For you will spread abroad to the right and to the left. And your descendants will possess nations and will resettle the desolate cities. Fear not, for you will not be put to shame; and do not feel humiliated, for you will not be disgraced; but you will forget the shame of your youth, and the reproach of your widowhood you will remember no more. For your Husband is your Maker, whose name is the Lord of Hosts; and your Redeemer is the Holy One of Israel, Who is called the God of All the Earth.*

For the Lord has called you, like a wife forsaken and grieved in spirit, even like a wife of one's youth when she is rejected," says your God. "For a brief moment I forsook you, but with great compassion and grace I will gather you. In an outburst of anger, I hid My face from you for a moment, but with everlasting lovingkindness I will have compassion on you," says the Lord your redeemer. "For this is like the days of Noah to Me, when I swore that the waters of Noah would not flood the earth again; so I have sworn that I will not be angry with you nor will I rebuke you. For the mountains may be removed and the hills may shake, but My lovingkindness will not be removed from you, and My covenant of peace will not be shaken," says the Lord who has compassion on you. "O afflicted one, storm-tossed, and not comforted, Behold, I will set your stones in antimony, and your foundations I will lay in sapphires. Moreover, I will make your battlements of rubies, and your gates of crystal, and your entire wall of precious stones. All your sons will be taught of the Lord; and the well-being of your sons will be great. In righteousness you will be established; you will be far from oppression, for you will not fear; terror will not come near you. If anyone fiercely assails you, it will not be from Me. Whoever assails you will fall because of you. Behold, I Myself have created the smith who blows the fire of coals and brings out a weapon for its work; and I have created the destroyer to ruin. No weapon that is formed against you will prosper; and every tongue that accuses you in judgement you will condemn. This is the heritage of the servants of the Lord, and their vindication is from me," declares the Lord.

Like the transformed butterfly emerging from its chrysalises, we will become known for the development of a beautiful, new and Christlike identity. Like Peter, Ezekiel, Moses and Jabez, it is time for every area in our life to expand and prosper.

CHAPTER NINE

A New Identity

When things are seen, known and understood by the heart, the truth of God's Word releases a dimension of revelation knowledge that spiritually renews the mind. *And the peace of God, which surpasses all understanding, will guard your hearts* (imagination) *and minds through Christ Jesus* (Philippians 4:7). As we learned previously, the word understanding means to go before time has happened into a higher, more advanced future realm of the Spirit. This is made possible so that we may gain spiritual understanding that will give us the wisdom, insight and power to correctly interpret that which is yet to come.

Spiritual understanding empowers us to be the person who is already prepositioned, waiting in the renewed state of mind and discerning where the glory or favor of the Lord is going to fall. *Keep your heart with all diligence, for out of the imagination spring the issues of life* (Proverbs 4:23).

The desires of your heart are not generated based on your need; they are believed, imagined, sketched, painted and then revealed. We behold what has been revealed by the releasing of our faith. Desires are, therefore, manifested by an inner faith that a new identity already exists within us.

When we agree with God's Word, the images of our newly-created man that God projects becomes the truth that remolds and sustains us. Positive, life-giving thoughts produce our inner speech. That inner speech exhorts and builds us up to do the greater works and actions. Our affirmative meditations on God's will construct a beautiful world of love, peace and acceptance—a world where creativity, prosperity, salvation, healing and deliverance are the norm.

When we are aware of God's higher ways, we can initiate changes in our imagination that will manifest the reality of our dreams and desires by releasing them into our waking world. The waking words of God's ancient wisdom we apply in our life will transform us. Signs always follow our conscious belief in God; signs never precede our faith by compelling things to materialize. Faith is the key.

When things are seen, known and understood by the heart, the truth of God's Word releases a dimension of revelation knowledge that spiritually renews the mind.

Things manifest when we have imagined, focused on and believed them to be so. God consciousness and our own spiritual awareness give us the power to decree that which will manifest—IAM healed, IAM rich, IAM prosperous, IAM more than enough, IAM loved and content, IAM strong. IAM able to do All Things through Christ who loves me and gave Himself for me. Therefore, IAM at rest!

When we embrace these statements of IAM as actual facts, our faith draws them out of the realm of our spirit. The faith facts we believe come alive to rest in us. Faith facts become a component of our consciousness. That God-conscious part of us can impress our subconscious with the truth of these faith facts. These spiritual truths are received into the imagination, incubated and nurtured by the subconscious until they are birthed in our consciousness as a new creation in our life. The person with a creative imagination births the visions of the unknown, bringing the invisible realms of creation into focus so that it can become a reality.

Jesus Christ is made manifest in the depths of our spirit, and we are transformed by being in His presence. We are converted by seeing and mirroring His image. Christ lovingly touches the soul so that He can move through the body of flesh—for IAM His beloved, and He is mine.

Jesus said:

> IAM the Door for the sheep (John 10:7).
>
> IAM the Door (John 10:9).
>
> IAM the Light of the World (John 8:12).
>
> IAM the Good Shepherd (John 10:).
>
> IAM the Bread of Life (John 6:35).
>
> IAM the Resurrection and the Life (John 11:25).
>
> IAM the Way, the Truth and the Life (John 14:6).
>
> IAM the True Vine (John 15:1).
>
> IAM the Alpha and Omega (Revelation 1:8).

IAM is not just a name. The word *am* is a state of being verb. IAM is what God does. The IAMs of God empower us to manifest the divine aspects of God. It is necessary to take on the divine nature of God so that we can be overcomers, those that eat of the hidden spiritual manna. The IAM of God becomes whatever He needs to be for us at any given moment. The IAM of God living in and through us empowers us to be whatever the Holy Spirit needs for us to be.

God's presence gives us command over more influence and authority than we have ever known. When the Spirit of God enlightens us, we are ready to learn how to increase, multiply and mature. The Holy Spirit grants us the ability to understand how to move beyond the gifting level and into spiritual maturity in love. He gives us the capability to be full of enough love to be mantled with the overflowing fullness of the office level of the Seven Spirits of God. *In the light of the king's face is life, and his favor is like* (the face of God hidden in) *a cloud of the latter rain* (Proverbs 16:15).

> *When we embrace these statements of IAM as actual facts, our faith draws them out of the realm of our spirit.*

Goodbye Old, Hello New

In two different, yet correlating, dreams one night, God revealed to me the necessity to shift into (function in) Christ's identity, where all limitations are removed:

> In my first dream, I was at an airport preparing to travel. There were officials (I later discerned the officials were angels) stationed at the boarding gate. When I approached to board the aircraft, the officials would not let me pass through the gate. The angelic authorities took my purse and confiscated my driver's license, which represented my current identity—how I am perceived, known and seen.
>
> When they held my driver's license up to my face to validate my identity, one of the angelic guards kept repeating, "This is not you!"
>
> I argued with them and defended myself, "IAM, indeed, Barbie Breathitt! IAM Dr. Barbie L. Breathitt." I persistently stated my case over and over again.
>
> While still dreaming, I finally diagnosed that if I wanted to move through the new gate to gain access into a higher, more powerful realm of spiritual flight, I would have to take on a new name and identity. Just like Moses, the Great IAM that IAM must send me to the leaders of the world. By taking on one or more of the IAMs of God, I would be embracing an expansive, ever-broadening and Christ-like identity. I needed a new name written down in glory before the angels would allow me to advance into a higher dimension of favor.
>
> In order to get on board with God's new agenda (to take off into the heavenly realms, to change atmospheres), I needed to be conformed into the image, likeness and nature of Christ. I needed to learn how to correctly discern and utilize the wisdom and power of Christ found in the different names of God.

> The angels then said to me, "Those who truly and intimately know their God shall be strong and do great exploits" (see Daniel 11:32).

If we do not even know His name—His hundreds of different names, characteristics and attributes of God and how to utilize each of them in our life—then how can we claim we know God? As I mentioned previously, we are a people who have become far too familiar with a God who we barely know! Without the proper and constant use of our imagination, we will never come to know the magnificence of God.

> In my second dream that night, I was staying at a hotel (place of transition). I ordered and ate dinner in the hotel restaurant. I wanted to charge my meal bill to my room, but the restaurant officials (angels) would not let me without presenting my identification. I realized I had left everything—my purse, identification, luggage and room key—in my hotel room.
>
> I proceeded to the front desk, so I could ask the clerk for another key. The desk clerk (angel) would not give me an additional key to gain entrance into my room without some proof of identity. They wanted an ID that would prove who IAM. I kept telling them that my luggage (which represents elegant gifts, not baggage) and driver's license (authority to operate a vehicle) were safely locked in the hotel room (temporary dwelling place). I told the clerk that in order to prove my identity, I needed access to my hotel room.
>
> By then, so much time had passed that it was already time to rush to the airport (a place that launches you into the airways to tap into global frequencies for media communications). I needed to leave so that I would not miss my departure flight (promotion that gives you very high visibility). It was absolutely necessary to have access to my hotel room to retrieve my luggage and personal belongings. *"For I know the plans I have for you," declares the Lord, "plans to prosper you and not to harm you, plans to give you hope and a future"* (Jeremiah 29:11).

> I knew this jet was going to take me to a brand new, higher destination (destiny). *Therefore, if any person is engrafted in Christ, the Messiah, he or she is a new creation, a new being altogether; the old, previous moral and spiritual condition has passed away. Behold, the fresh and new has come* (2 Corinthians 5:17).
>
> The angelic clerk would not believe me when I declared, "IAM Dr. Barbie L. Breathitt!" I could not gain access into my hotel room without becoming someone new in Christ. It became obvious it was past time to take on one of His names (characteristics, attributes) and to emerge on stage as a new creation with my new IAM identity.

God is building His powerful army from the specially-trained ops, team members of the Triumphant Reserve. These Dread Champions have forgotten the former things and do not consider the old ways of doing things. Kingdom guardians must perceive, behold and know the new thing that is springing forth, and they must give heed to it. God has made a way in the wilderness for the deep wells within our bellies to make rivers in the dry, desert valleys of decision so that we can give drink to those He has chosen and formed for Himself to declare His high praises (see Isaiah 43:15–21).

Kingdom guardians must perceive, behold and know the new thing that is springing forth, and they must give heed to it.

CHAPTER TEN

Sometimes You Have to Fly Solo

Those who have traveled with us up to this point may not be able to continue with us into the depths and spiritual heights where God is leading us during this superior, highly advanced transitional era. New systems, structures and identities must be established to carry us to the broad domains of exposure, splendid mansions and kingdom estates that God has prepared for us to enter into and possess.

> *He who loves and takes more joy and pleasure in their father or mother more than Me is not worthy of Me. And he who loves son or daughter more than Me is not worthy of Me. And he who does not take his cross, crucify himself by constantly cleaving to My example of living and follow after Me is not worthy of Me* (Matthew 10:37–38).

One must be overshadowed with God's presence to become pregnant with a higher purpose and far-reaching destiny. His imposing manifestation gives each of us a striking vision and major determination for our life. The Holy Spirit is intentionally activating the spiritual gifts to function at a mystifying level. He is multiplying anointings and expanding the presentation of the buried talents that are currently hidden within each of us. God's rushing river currents flowing through our dry, barren places will unearth the jeweled treasures that have been covered. God's shining light will illuminate the diamonds' many brilliant faucets.

God is accessing our veiled gifts, genius endowments and unseen capabilities in order to magnify all of our unknown abilities to bring glory unto Him. He does this by encouraging us to submit to taking a higher, different and most difficult spiritual road. At different points in our life, God places a demand on everything He has invested in us. For us to move effectively in an area where we are inexperienced, we need to develop a greater measure of trust in God. Then we must yield to the breath of His Spirit. *God gave Abraham this command: "Leave your own country. Leave your family, relatives and your inheritance. Move into unknown territory, where I will show you a new regional homeland"* (Acts 7:3).

When we follow God in a new direction, we travel into an expansive territory that carries us beyond man's opinions, especially those of our own household. Family sees us after the flesh, in our weaknesses as we grew older. They do not see or honor the spiritual callings and giftings God has placed upon us. To enter into God's grand desires and to possess His unique designs for our life, we must avoid the formula for failure—trying to please people. Leave the fear of man in the dust of your past. If you want to be the orchestra leader of the new and harmonious sound, you must be willing to turn your back to a certain crowd of people.

God is accessing our veiled gifts, genius endowments and unseen capabilities in order to magnify all of our unknown abilities to bring glory unto Him.

Separation from Family

> *Jesus said, "Truly I tell you, there is no one who has given up and left house or brothers or sisters or mother or father or children or lands for My sake and for the gospel's who will not receive a hundred times as much now in this time—houses and brothers and sisters and mothers and children and lands, with persecutions—and in the age to come, eternal life"* (Mark 10:29–30).

Abraham, Joseph and Jacob all had to leave their family in order to accomplish their destiny. Abraham lost the best of his inheritance to his brother-in-law, Lot, because he brought Lot with him when he wasn't supposed to. Joseph's brothers were jealous of him because their father favored him.

They despised, hated and sabotaged Joseph for decreeing his dreams of grandeur.

Family rarely sees and honors the God-potential in other family members, because they know them after the carnal flesh, not by the spirit. We've either heard of or personally experienced these family dynamics at some point in our life. We frequently hear of a wife complaining about her meddling mother-in-law. Sometimes, in-laws can feel threatened by and resentful or jealous of the close relationships between birth brothers and sisters, which divides, hurts and further separates family members. Even Jesus experienced separation from His earthly family. The Son of God was viewed by His brothers as just another sibling. And His mother Mary saw and often treated Jesus just as a son, not as the Messiah.

> *Someone said to Jesus, "Listen! Your mother and Your brothers are standing outside, seeking to speak to You." But Jesus replied to the man who told Him, "Who is My mother, and who are My brothers?" And stretching out His hand toward not only the twelve disciples but all His adherents, Jesus said, "Here are My mother and My brothers. For whoever does the will of My Father in heaven is My brother and sister and mother"* (Matthew 10: 47–50)*!*

Evolution of Change

To enter into the blessing found in the ever-expanding family of God, one must first experience the separation from Egypt (world) and sin. You must then embrace your calling unto God and incorporate Him into every aspect of your life. Then you transition yourself into an even higher platform of faith by moving through the dark transformational tunnel. The transformational tunnel is where one learns to reincorporate God into his or her new, Christlike identity at a much higher level. Looking back causes stagnation, so you must keep going forward. If you ever stop, Pharaoh will overtake and capture you.

To enter into the blessing found in the ever-expanding family of God, one must first experience the separation from Egypt (world) and sin.

The cutting of the flesh is painful (see Joshua 5). After circumcision, one has to distance himself from others for a time of healing. During your time of healing, never look back in regret to preserve the past, or your progress will be paralyzed (at a standstill) as a pillar of salt. Do not stare into the rearview mirror, but learn to work through and cut off emotional attachments.

Pray for a clear vision that has the power to pull you out of your present circumstances into a successfully designed future. Make the attraction of the future greater than the memories of the past. Do not allow emotional attachments to rule over or void your opportunities.

The transformational tunnel is dark. There are no lights, but we must keep moving—even if we are stumbling forward, slowly testing every step with toe-tapping that feels for bumps, lumps and landmines buried in the ground.

The easy, broad door of compromise yields very little reward or produce; it often leads to the destruction of your highest destiny.

His eyes are on the ways of mortals; He sees their every step (Job 34:21).

Nevertheless, the righteous will hold to their ways, and those with clean hands will grow stronger (Job 17:9).

We cannot see our way ahead, because God is developing our capacity to walk in a higher dimension of faith, not by sight. *But He knows the way that I take; when He has tested me, I will come forth as gold* (Job 23:10).

I will teach you about the power of God; the ways of the Almighty I will not conceal (Job 27:11).

Keep prayerfully inching forward toward the door.

> *Good and upright is the Lord; therefore He instructs sinners in His ways. He guides the humble in what is right and teaches them His way. All the ways of the Lord are loving and faithful toward those who keep the demands of His covenant* (Psalm 25:8–10).

On our way to beyond, Satan will throw everything at us to stop our progress. *There are those who rebel against the light, who do not know its ways or stay in its paths* (Job 24:13).

Personal Reflection Moment

1. Take an accurate inventory of where you are currently.
2. Are you moving forward, even if it's an army crawl? Or are you stagnant or shrinking back?
3. What doors are before you?
4. Now identify and discern where you are going. God has gone before you. He has already ordained the narrow and higher path to breakthrough!

During seasons of change, be very intentional in discerning the steps to take and the new doors to enter. Always choose the door with the most adversity in order to experience the greatest harvest and to collect the most fruit. The easy, broad door of compromise yields very little reward or produce; if selected it often leads to the destruction of your highest destiny.

When we arrive at the end of the transformational tunnel, many effectual doors will open. It is wisdom to choose the most foreboding door, for an effectual door is always marked by many adversaries. Satan will decorate his door with glittering limelight that appeals to the flesh. If chosen, this door will lead to a dead end.

Israel had to separate from Egypt and be delivered (from slave mentality) into freedom as they went through the tunnel of the Red Sea. From there, they entered the wilderness wanderings to discover the provision and protection of God. By crossing over the Jordan River, Israel entered into their Promised Land. Eight spies released an evil eye (*rah*) report of death, while only two released a good (*tov*) report of life. Believing a bad report caused them to miss out on their promises and to wander aimlessly in the desert for forty years of judgment.

> *After we step through the door of adversity to conquer our enemies, people will call us the Sons of God.*

Elisha had to leave and separate himself from the school of the prophets.

He went through the Jordan River with Elijah. Elijah separated from Elisha when he was taken up into heaven by the whirlwind-driven chariot of horses. Elisha picked up Elijah's discarded mantle and used it to cross back over the Jordan River. Elisha had to return wearing and moving in the power of Elijah's mantle before those who knew him as a lowly servant could recognize him as a new man of authority. Before Elisha returned to stand before his peers at the school of the prophets, he had taken on his leadership role. Elisha incorporated his new identity as the institute's head, senior-most prophet.

> *But now, in spite of past judgments for Israel's sins, thus says the Lord, He who created you, O Jacob, and He who formed you, O Israel: "Fear not, for I have redeemed you; ransomed by paying a price instead of leaving you as a captive; I have called you by your name; You are mine"* (Isaiah 43:1).

Jacob's first identity was created and known by his family who named him as a worldly deceiver and supplanter. But God said, "Israel, I have formed a new identity for you that will shift you into a new, dynamic kingdom." Jacob took off his relatives' old (flesh) label to put on his new (heavenly) garments and princely identity as Israel.

We cannot advance in the identity of who the world says we are. We must stop answering yes to old structures and labels. Cut off familiar, fleshly relationships, and circumcise the flesh to enter into the new identity of IAM in Christ. Say yes to the new, God-given family, friends, lands and identity God has created and formed for you.

> *As we acknowledge God's presence, we make more room for Him to move in powerful, profound ways in and through us.*

Light shines brighter and brighter in the higher dimension of promotion. Faith increases our spiritual strength, while glory takes us higher and higher. Once we have evolved into the new creature God has ordained and created us to become, people look up and respond to us much differently. Honor and favor come because we are manifesting a new glory that carries something of God they have never seen. After we step through the door of adversity to conquer our enemies, people will call us the Sons of God.

When a man finds his enemy, does he let him get away unharmed? May the Lord reward you well for the way you treated me today (1 Samuel 24:19).

Then Saul said to David, "May you be blessed, David my son; you will do great things and surely triumph." So, David went on his way, and Saul returned home (1 Samuel 26:25).

The loving God who created the universe also lives largely within and among us. As we acknowledge God's presence, we make more room for Him to move in powerful and profound ways in and through us. *Now, if anyone is enfolded into Christ, he has become an entirely new creation. All that is related to the old order has vanished. Behold, everything is fresh and new* (2 Corinthians 5:17).

CHAPTER ELEVEN

IAM His Beloved

God is the great IAM of eternity. When I dwell in the transforming power of the great IAM, I discover my new name (which no man knows, except me) is IAM. IAM no longer my own, but I have been hidden within the glory of Christ Jesus, because (the verb) IAM that IAM has sent me (see Revelation 2:17). Jesus and His Father are united as one glorious being (see John 10:30). *If you had known Me, you would have known My Father also; and from now on you know Him and have seen Him* (John 14:7).

As Believers, we are also one body with God the Father and joint heirs with Jesus. *There is one body and one Spirit, just as you were called in one hope of your calling; one Lord, one faith, one baptism; one God and Father of all, who is above all, and through all, and in you all* (Ephesians 4:4–6).

IAM able to live, move and have my new being created in Christ. I stand with the spirit of my mind, having been renewed in Christ. IAM able to stay there in His presence. IAM situated. IAM bilocated. IAM knit together and growing up at rest in Him. Because IAM, I live, subsist. IAM alive (survive and thrive). IAM coexisting in Christ. IAM a physical and spiritual being. IAM and, therefore, good things happen, occur, transpire, befall, ensue, take place and come about. Because IAM abiding in Christ, they come to pass.

> *But, speaking the truth in love, may grow up in All Things into Him who is the head—Christ—from whom the whole*

> *body, joined and knit together by what every joint supplies, according to the effective working by which every part does its share, causes growth of the body for the edifying of itself in love. This I say, therefore, and testify in the Lord, that you should no longer walk as the rest of the Gentiles walk, in the futility of their mind, having their understanding darkened, being alienated from the life of God, because of the ignorance that is in them, because of the blindness of their heart; who, being past feeling, have given themselves over to lewdness, to work all uncleanness with greediness. But you have not so learned Christ, if indeed you have heard Him and have been taught by Him, as the truth is in Jesus: that you put off, concerning your former conduct, the old man which grows corrupt according to the deceitful lusts, and be renewed in the spirit of your mind, and that you put on the new man which was created according to God, in true righteousness and holiness. Therefore, putting away lying. Let each one of you speak truth with his neighbor, for we are members of one another. Be angry, and do not sin. Do not let the sun go down on your wrath, nor give place to the devil* (Ephesians 4:15–26).

We know God the Father by what we see the IAM doing. When we behold IAM, we are transformed into His image to become the portion of the IAM that He needs us to be. As Barbie, IAM a prophet, IAM a teacher, IAM a preacher, IAM an evangelist and IAM an apostle. IAM an ambassador for God, IAM a friend of God and IAM a disciple of Christ. IAM a healer, IAM a creative miracle worker and IAM a deliverer. IAM a business woman, IAM an entrepreneur and IAM a professional. IAM becoming All Things to all men so that I may win some to Christ.

We know God the Father by what we see the IAM doing.

> *For though IAM free from all men, I have made myself a servant to all, that I might win the more; and to the Jews I became as a Jew, that I might win Jews; to those who are under the law, I become as if IAM also under the law, that I might win those who are under the law; to those who are without*

> *law, I become as without law* (not being without law toward God but under law toward Christ), *that I might win those who are without law; to the weak I became as weak, that I might win the weak. I have become All Things to all men that I might by all means save some. Now this I do for the gospel's sake, that I may be partaker of it with you* (1 Corinthians 9:19–23).

The IAM of God arises in me to indicate the center concept of my existence. IAM Barbie, a woman, a minister. IAM a friend, a daughter, a sister, a caregiver. IAM an author, an expert dream analyst, a life coach. But most of all, IAM a lover of God. All of these unique IAMs that IAM are representative parts and diverse concepts that make up the person of my whole being. When I realize that IAM exists, I enter into a permanent conscious awareness that IAM a diverse, complex being created in God's image. The type of IAM that IAM manifesting at that moment will determine my movements, actions and responses.

The IAM of God arises in me to indicate the center concept of my existence.

IAM able to arise to any occasion. IAM able to become whoever or whatever I need to be at any given instant. As noted in 1 Corinthians 9:22, Paul became as weak so that he might win the weak. No matter what form, function or action I take, IAM still the same (core) person. I have discovered whether IAM the *Good Samaritan*, the *Prophet* or the *Teacher*. With God's help, IAM the sculptor of my own unique world.

We learn to trust in God by resting upon the greatness of that particular portion of the IAM. When the Christ in us becomes the central part of our permanent awareness, we enter into rest. As we rest in the loving embrace of the Christ that is within, we discover there is nothing impossible for us when we work as joint heirs with Christ.

This newfound success in the IAM empowers the Believer to do God's will. We enter into the door that is only found in Jesus Christ in order to go into His presence. We draw out of Christ the divine knowledge that empowers us to create spiritual wealth so that we are spiritually, physically, emotionally and financially free (see Psalm 46:1).

The Spirit of God galvanizes us to serve the Kingdom of God and man in any capacity that is needed. The Holy Spirit teaches us how to enter into Jesus in order to rest in the Lord. We become a doorkeeper in God's presence. One day of intimacy within the Father's heart is better than a thousand days spent in the most beautiful palaces of the wicked on earth. Just standing in front of Jesus (the Gate Beautiful) causes our heart to sing, rejoice and worship God (see Psalm 84:10).

Within the chambers of the Father's heart, we open the door of our heart (imagination) to see Him standing in our presence, to hear His voice and to feel His desires as He shares intimate secrets of His heart. We see how to manifest God's glory in order to bring His perfect will into existence. In this holy place, the IAM God enters in and shares a feast of wisdom and insights with us, so we are changed into His reflective likeness. *The Spirit of the Lord will come powerfully upon you, and you will prophesy with them; and you will be changed into a different person* (1 Samuel 10:6).

The miracle power of Christ's imagination is actively dwelling within our subconscious mind. *And God said, "This is the token of the covenant* (solemn pledge) *which IAM making between Me and you and every living creature that is with you, for all future generations"* (Genesis 9:12).

The sanctified imagination heals every one of our negative states of being by removing the dark, broken thoughts of lack. The indwelling power of Christ surrounds and transforms us by renewing our mind with the truth found in the power of His Word. The light of God's truth replaces the dark falsehoods that previously distorted, blocked and crippled our thought processes.

Being conscious of our access to the mind of Christ empowers us to be delivered from all spiritual, material, emotional and physical bondages.

When the life-giving Word of God renews our mind, we discover that the needed states (mansions) of happiness, health and wealth were always present and just waiting to be recognized, chosen and occupied by us. When we were in our blinded state, we were not able to see Jesus, the door of entrance.

But whoever hates a fellow Believer lives in the darkness—stumbling around in the dark with no clue where he is going, for he is blinded by the darkness (1 John 2:11).

God has blinded their eyes and hardened their hearts to the truth. So with their eyes and hearts closed they cannot understand the truth nor turn to Me so that I could instantly cleanse and heal them (John 12:40).

For their minds have been blinded by the god of this age, leaving them in unbelief. Their blindness keeps them from seeing the dayspring light of the wonderful news of the glory of Jesus Christ, who is the divine image of God (2 Corinthians 4:4).

Their corrupted logic has been clouded because their hearts are so far from God—their blinded understanding and deep-seated moral darkness keeps them from the true knowledge of God (Ephesians 4:18).

Truth spiritually renews and liberates the mind from its prison. Locked doors that have blocked our way are sprung wide open. Being conscious of our access to the mind of Christ empowers us to be delivered from all spiritual, material, emotional and physical bondages. Having been saved, healed and delivered, we become the deliverers that open the prison doors to set other captives free (see Isaiah 61:1).

Moses was the greatest deliverer in history, second only to Jesus. Moses set a whole nation of slaves free from the bondage of Egypt (the world's darkness). *And God said to Moses, "IAM WHO IAM." And He said, "Thus you shall say to the children of Israel, IAM has sent me to you"* (Exodus 3:14).

Imagination: A Tool not a Toy

Properly guided through gates,
Guarded by haloed hands
Becomes a tool of life-directed force
For good of all mankind.
. . . missed, only a toy of fools.

Keat Wade 05/05/19 (30 Nissan 5779)

CHAPTER TWELVE

IAM—A New Name!

I received a new identity and was forever changed in February of 2018. I was in the Spirit on the Lord's Day when I had an open vision:

> A massive, ancient lock suspended in the air appeared before me. The Holy Spirit invited me to enter into the heart-shaped lock through the skeleton key opening on the front of the lock. When I approached the keyhole, it was like a large, arched entryway into a castle or fortress. The entryway was plenty big enough for me to walk through.
>
> The arched walkway led into the intricate inner workings of a massive lock. I realized that the presence and the active movements of my body were being used as keys to gain entrance into the depths of the various chambers of the giant lock.
>
> Once inside the lock, I had to learn how to move in new, varied and diverse ways in order to advance within the internal gears, workings and different compartments, legislative and judicial chambers and boardrooms of the lock. There were times when I needed to prophesy, decree or declare to advance through a tumbler. When I did, I achieved entrance into halls or assembly rooms. Other times I had to sing, rejoice, praise or worship, releasing a new and dif-

ferent sound or frequency, in order to open the doors into a new hall, room or passageway. At times I had to be silent, enter into peace and still my spirit until it could rest in God's presence in order to hear and see what the Father was doing.

When I was given vision, I was also given clear direction through a word of knowledge, wisdom and counsel on how to advance and which steps to take. Sometimes the weight of the Kabod glory resting on me would trigger a lock to open when I simply stood in reverent awe, bowed low in respect or laid down in honor of God's presence. The weight of God's glorious presence pressed Him into me. At various times, angels appeared to give me a specific tool, anointing or word that was required to turn the gears to open the next door.

Within the intricate workings of the lock, I stood before what looked like an impenetrable, massive castle door that was fortified with iron bands. I didn't have the key to open the lock. God said to me, "In the presence of a locked door, do not back down or take no for an answer! I have given you free reign in My Kingdom with no restrictions. I have gone before you to clear a paved path. I have given you the power to break down bronze gates, smash locks and kick down barred entrances" (see Psalm 45:2; 107:16).

Immediately upon my agreement with God's command to not take no for an answer, a well-equipped, leather tool belt appeared around my waist. I chose a large, sturdy screwdriver and took it out of the holster. I inserted the flat blade under the door's hinges. I was able to remove the door's hinge pins from their secure places. With the ease of supernatural strength, I easily lifted and quickly removed the massive door from its hinges and slid it to the side. This left a huge, broad opening through which I advanced. The Lord spoke to me, "Now, that is a door no man can shut" (see Isaiah 45:1–3).

These are the words of the Holy One, the True One, He Who

> *has the key of David, Who opens and no one shall shut, Who shuts and no one shall open: I know your record of works and what you are doing. See! I have set before you a door wide open which no one is able to shut; I know that you have but little power, and yet you have kept My Word and guarded My message and have not renounced or denied My name* (Revelation 3:7–8).
>
> From there, the mouth of God gave me a brand new name. The name Dr. Barbie L. Breathitt could only take me so far. Any residue of past lack, rejection, failure, shame, guilt, weakness or ruin was stripped from me. An angel's voice then said, "You are God's chosen because you have acknowledged Him. He has armed you with strength for a privileged work. He calls you a pillar, even though there are so many ways in which you do not currently know Him. Still, it is His great delight to give you a royal crown of the Kingdom (see Isaiah 62). As you take on this new covenant identity of love and authority, the attributes, characteristics and the power that is resident in the hundreds of names of Christ must emerge from within you."
>
> After a candlelit marriage ceremony (candles represent the romantic light of the soul), I was overshadowed by the identity of Christ. The IAM of God became the major part of me because IAM centered in Christ Jesus.

Once IAM aware of being centered in Christ, by taking on His image and likeness, whoever I need to be, IAM. IAM the Bride of Christ, who is called to clothe herself in her wedding garments. IAM His Beloved, and He is mine. IAM created in His image to mirror His likeness, so IAM a miracle worker. IAM healed, therefore, IAM a healer. IAM saved, so I can heal, deliver and save others from their sin through the name and blood of the Living Word.

> Christ gave me a stunning crown of light. We shared communion together; we drank from a golden-jeweled goblet. We tasted both an ancient wine and sipped the best of a new wine. Jesus and I walked hand in hand down endless corridors. He showed me the vast wealth of my inheritance

(which was concealed in innumerable chambers and buried with mounds of treasures) that is waiting for me. Each costly gem and every precious jewel represented another inestimable gift or irreplaceable spiritual ability He has stored up to give to His triumphant Bride.

Suddenly, the IAM part of God dwelling within me gave me understanding of the depths of mysteries, as untold secrets were revealed to me. The IAM in me could read the ancient writings found on the Scrolls of Wisdom. The IAM within me was given books of knowledge to study. God's glory empowered me to know the secrets, thoughts and intents of people's hearts.

This God of Light has no equal or rival. He created and holds the future of every individual person in His loving hands. God also embraces the destiny of every sheep and goat nation in His hand. The choices you make and actions you take form the attitudes you adopt. Your beliefs, choices, ways of thinking and actions can and will alter your malleable future, for IAM (you are) a Son of God.

When we identify ourself with God's desires, His surrounding presence will continually rest in us to fully grant the manifestation of our heart's requests.

The concepts and opinions I hold as truth about myself will determine my experiences in life. If I develop a higher self-concept, I will experience a different, higher future. Any adopted belief will form a person's self-concepts. Our mindset directs and determines our actions that form our world. Our beliefs have a creative force. We can consciously change our future by taking on the mind of Christ. His higher thoughts, ways and desires motivate us to actions that will overcome any perceived limitation by creating a different, better outcome.

After beholding the immeasurable inheritance awaiting me, I pressed on. My determined goal kept me moving forward and toward the center of the lock. Suddenly, I was made aware that from the backside of the lock, heaven and the angelic realm were mirroring my every move. I saw the kingdom of heaven advancing to meet me at the center

> point. The forces of heaven and my spiritually-awakened, earthen vessel met in the middle of the lock. The Holy Spirit then revealed to me that the lock was actually the pulsating chambers of my heavenly Father's heart.
>
> As I had ascended past the good and acceptable measures of God's will into His perfect plan, I had been trained, equipped and transformed within the Father's heart. Increase turned into multiplication as I had progressed through the various levels, ladders and chambers to reach the center of God's perfect will. During my journey, Holy Spirit revealed God as love. The Holy Spirit displayed the different aspects of Christ's names, His characteristics and both His concealed and revealed power of the divine attributes of His nature. His presence contained and brought out both the old and the new.
>
> Upon reaching the middle foundation of God's heart (imagination), I understood that I was centered within Christ Jesus, seated with Him on His throne in heavenly places. I knew I could ask of God whatever my heart (imagination) desired, and it would be granted to me.

When we identify ourself with God's desires, His surrounding presence will continually rest in us to fully grant the manifestation of our heart's requests.

> God's throne was alive and moving on wheels that were carried by awesome winged creatures. These heavenly beings were breathing out living praise and worship. These awe-inspiring beings were covered with beautiful eyes looking in every direction into interdimensional, spiritual territories all at the same time. I, too, could see, perceive and know the depths of mysteries. The spirit moving within me was mature because it followed in perfect harmony with the centrality of God. It was then that I could understand what is written in the Bible: *God has both raised up the Lord Jesus and will also raise us up by His power* (1 Corinthians 6:14).

Dream encounters help us see our destiny from God's perspective, so they have a lasting transformational effect on us. Dream encounters bring us to a new level of spiritual understanding. So we can sit with Christ in the place He has gone before us to prepare.

God has blessed us in all spiritual blessings when we are seated together with Christ as joint heirs in heavenly places (Ephesians 2:6).

We are not the ones who construct this heavenly ladder, but we must learn to ascend by discovering who we are in Christ. When we lift Jesus up, He will draw all men unto Himself. We climb the rungs of *Jacob's Ladder* by daily dying to the negative aspects of ourself. When we repent of the critical thoughts that we possess toward ourself and others, we will continue to ascend. By taking up the rugged cross of Christ and vertically lifting Jesus up from the earth, we make Jesus the focal point that draws our intentional focus to His beautiful face and all men unto His perfect, life-saving love (see John 12:32).

> *Through knowing how to operate our gifts, accepting our callings and then manifesting God's impending, purposed goals for us, we are able to carry out the imminent, forthcoming plans of heaven on earth now.*

The greatest power in the universe is love, which is only found in God's Kingdom of Love! We know that Jesus stands at the top of the ladder, as the heavenly door of access, to grant us more of an awareness of His Father. Jesus is the one who gives us entrance into the dimensions of heaven's spiritual reality. Jesus is the only truthful way to eternal life. *Let the morning bring me word of Your unfailing love, for I have put my trust in You. Show me the way I should go, for to You I entrust my life* (Psalm 143:8).

I have kept all the ways of the Lord; never turning my heart from the Lord. How skilled you are at pursuing love! Even the worst of women can learn from your ways (Jeremiah 2:33).

As for God, His way is perfect: The Lord's Word is flawless; He shields all who take refuge in Him (2 Samuel 22:22, 31).

...Lord, God of Israel, there is no God like You in heaven above or on earth below. You keep Your covenant of love with Your servants who continue whole-

heartedly in Your ways (1 Kings 8:23).

The Spirit of God gives us access to properly discern reality, obtain the forgiveness of sin and receive God's love. The Spirit of God gives us the power to see the Kingdom of God by manifesting His glory. Our sustained imagination creates the ability for us to see ourself being anything we desire to become. Through knowing how to operate our gifts, accepting our callings and then manifesting God's impending, purposed goals for us, we are able to carry out the imminent, forthcoming plans of heaven on earth now.

CHAPTER THIRTEEN

Advancing in the Levels of Glory

It is the measure of understanding of the revelation that we hold of Christ dwelling in us that determines what level of glory we can access and ascend to. It also determines which dimension of glory that we are empowered to abide in and maintain. God will not share His glory with another who has a different nature or spirit. But we are not another. Believers are one with Christ—if we possess the divine nature of God by becoming Sons of God.

The whole earth is crying out for the manifestation of the Sons of God! *IAM the eternal One. IAM the Lord, IAM is My name. My beauty is unique, a weighty splendor all My own. And nothing else, no idols could possibly gain My praise. My glory I will not give to another, nor My praise to carved images* (Isaiah 42:8).

But it is all on account of Me, not of you, that I act, for My own sake, for My own sake, I will do it that I retain honor; that My glory is Mine alone, and not sullied, for how should My name be profaned? And I will not give My glory to another (Isaiah 48:11).

As we mature in the knowledge of God by renewing our mind, we gain deeper spiritual insights into the ways of God. We can move out of functioning in our gifts in the anointing realm and graduate into moving in His glory. When we are touched by the manifestation of the Holy Spirit, the Spirit of Wisdom and His divine Knowledge and Understanding train and Counsel us to know how to respond to and minister in the Spirit of Might.

Always keep your eyes focused on what the Spirit of God is doing. He is our teacher; never look to man for promotion. *The wise shall inherit glory: but shame shall be the promotion of fools* (Proverbs 3:35).

Lift up your eyes to God; for your help, salvation and promotion come from the Lord. He will rescue and prosper you in a new way. For promotion cometh neither from the east, nor from the west, nor from the south. But God is the judge: He puts down one and exalts another (Psalm 75:6–7).

If we have ever once been caught up by or gone somewhere in the Spirit, ascended a heavenly ladder or even imagined being in heavenly places, our soul has memorized that path, so we can easily return to that spiritual dimension over and over again. *But the path of the just is like the shining sun, that shines ever brighter unto the perfect day* (Proverbs 4:18). Just as a mighty river traces the same path flowing safely within its banks, our soul learns to flow in the Spirit to reach the Spirit of God. *All the rivers run into the sea, yet the sea is not full; to the place from which the rivers come, there they return again* (Ecclesiastes 1:7).

For us to achieve our dreams, goals and destiny in life, we must allow the inner workings of the imagination to believe God and to see, retain and develop a higher path of action.

Because our natural, physical man appears to be more real to the touch, we falsely consider him to be the real person. This outer, physical shell of our body is used to house the extreme expanse of our eternal spirit and the soul of our true, magnificent being.

For us to achieve our dreams, goals and destiny in life, we must allow the inner workings of the imagination to believe God and to see, retain and develop a higher path of action. Learning to walk by the movement of the Spirit removes us from the obligation we feel to obey physical sensations. Until we live by faith and continue to walk in the liberty of the Spirit of the Lord, we will not obtain the higher aims or mansions God has set before us.

Every journey begins with a dream, a vision or an idea that is formed from within the creative chambers of the imagination. When we close our physical eyes to see, our spiritual eyes will open to imagine the end result. Once the shift from the natural to the spiritual takes place, we are ready to take the first internal step.

The moving of the Spirit within us forges a higher path that motivates the will of our natural man to surrender to God and follow the leading of the Holy Spirit. *Every place that the sole of your foot will tread upon I have already given you* (Joshua 1:3).

The person we are currently is all we know and can see, so that person is all we can be. A sincere desire to change and become a different person will transform us into the image of Christ.

To advance spiritually, we must review the visions and dreams the Spirit of God has implanted or shown us in our imagination. A correct interpretation will empower our thoughts to expand in order to amend our attitudes and life accordingly. When our thoughts are refined and our attitudes are revised, our actions will create a life path that will achieve our visions. And the glory of God will manifest in us and through us!

The Creator has graciously given you the limitless gift of your imagination to know Him, to know His purposes and to be who He destined you to be. Dream BIG! Be BOLD! Mount up your wings and soar as Almighty approves you on! You can fully trust Him as the faithful wind beneath your wings. Rise up and march forth with the faith of God, and He will steadfastly back you up! *Imagine* the impossible—for nothing is impossible with God!

To advance spiritually, we must review the visions and dreams the Spirit of God has implanted or shown us in our imagination.

Let Us Pray

Dear Jesus, we welcome You to rule and reign as the supreme Lord and Savior of our lives. Teach us to rest in Your loving embrace, for You are truly the one and only Lord of all creation. Awaken our God-given imaginations. Show us how to obtain the kingdom keys that open our imaginations, so we can know You in Your grandeur.

We ask that the Spirit of the Lord would speak clearly to each and every one of us. Place Your Word upon our lips and on our tongues. Let it reside within our hearts. We long to be contrite of spirit so that everything that we do is compelled by the leading of the Holy Spirit. Help us to walk uprightly and tremble at Your words, so You can do good toward us. Let the Word of the Lord dwell in us richly in all wisdom, teaching us His ways so that we can admonish one another in psalms, hymns and spiritual songs, singing with grace in our hearts to You, Lord. Help us to comprehend spiritual truths, gain godly wisdom and walk in a higher level of revelation knowledge. Empower us to speak forth Your life-giving words with boldness in the miraculous demonstration of the Spirit's power.

We ask that You shake everything that can be shaken so that the things that remain in us are completely of You. Open new spiritual doors of opportunity so that we can enter into the boundless expanses of God. Bless us with every spiritual blessing as we ascend into the heavenly places in Christ. Empower us to transition out of carnal reasoning into the possessing of the mind of Christ.

Thank you for choosing, predestining and accepting us in the Beloved. Thank you for adopting us as sons from before the foundations of the world. Create in us a clean heart so that we are found to be holy, without blame, before You in love. Cause Your wisdom and prudence to abound toward us.

Help us to grow in prayer and meditation so that You can make known to us the mysteries of Your perfect will and good pleasure. We ask that You cause everything to work together for our good, because we love You. Redeem us through Your blood. Forgive our sins, and pour out the richness of Your grace upon us so we may be found pleasing in Your sight. Strengthen us for Your service. Seal us, those who believe and trust in You, with the promised power of Your Holy Spirit flowing in and through us as part of our inheritance.

We ask that You give us the Spirit of Wisdom and Revelation in the knowledge of Christ Jesus. Open the eyes of our understanding so that we are enlightened and may know the hope of Christ's calling, the exceeding greatness of His power toward us and the riches of the glory of His inheritance in the saints. Let the same power that resurrected Christ from the dead be alive and working within each one of us. We ask all these things in the wonderful, matchless name of Jesus Christ. Amen.

Author's Note

In the third volume of the *IMAGINE* series, we will persist to unwrap the marvelous design and workings of the supernatural imagination. Through Scripture, dreams, visions and the profound power of imaginative prayer and faith, we will continue to learn how to unlock the glory and complete authority of God in our life and throughout the nations. As you advance to procure and fully access the mind of Christ, you will be empowered to thoroughly activate your new identity, excel beyond third dimension limitations and fully exercise the realm of the Spirit.

About the Author

DR. BARBIE L. BREATHITT

DR. BARBIE BREATHITT is a certified prophetic life coach (AskBarbie.com), published best-selling author, dedicated educator and experienced revelatory teacher of the divine, supernatural manifestations of God, whose greatest desire is to see other reach, fullfill and enjoy their destiny in God. She is recognized around the world as a leading master dream analyst (DreamsDecoder.com) and healing evangelist with deliverance, signs, wonders and creative miracles following. Barbie's prophetic seer gifting and deep spiritual insights have helped and equipped thousands of people, including business, media and government leaders, and ministries in over 40 nations understand God's mystical ways.

Dr. Barbie Breathitt teaches individuals, trains corporate professionals and business teams, government leaders and churches how to recognize, respond to and release the activity of God with unique strategies. Her sincere pursuit of God's Kingdom and His eternal truth make Barbie's Texas-based Breath of the Spirit Ministries, Inc. a predominant worldwide foundation.

An experienced teacher, published author, prophetic voice, dream analyst and healing evangelist, she has released God's love, presence and breath in prisons, hospitals, streets, Europe, third-world nations, television, radio and the internet. Her deepest desire is to see people fulfill their unique destiny here on earth. Barbie's training, resources and personal ministry help others to interpret and apply the direction God gives them through encounters, dreams and visions.

Barbie Breathitt personally learned and now passionately teaches God's Love, Presence and Breath. Her astute prophetic voice and accurate dream analyses have blessed those in prisons, hospitals, Europe and third-world nations, enabling many hungry people to grow. Barbie has abandoned herself to the Holy Spirit with miracles, signs and wonders following. Many individuals have been miraculously healed in her meetings while others have experienced the Presence of the Spirit as never before. Her infectious humor promotes unity with those inside and outside the church walls.

An ordained healing evangelist, Barbie has ministered for over thirty-five years around the world. Barbie established and conducted three prophetic training centers. Barbie now lives in Texas and opened Breath of the Spirit Center of Training in 2004. Breath of the Spirit offers a variety of courses on Healing, Revelatory Gifts, Dream Interpretation and Evangelistic Outreaches.

SPEAKING ENGAGEMENTS

Traveling around the world to share wisdom and insights regarding sound, biblical dream interpretation, Barbie is available for conferences, teaching and hands-on training. Please contact Barbie's ministry at Breath of the Spirit Ministries, Inc. through email (info@DreamsDecoder.com), the website (DreamsDecoder.com) or by phone at (972) 253-6653 for more information.

The *IMAGINE* Series

Volume I will help you understand and fully comprehend that the Spirit of Christ dwells mightily within your sanctified imagination. Discover how to supplant the carnal mindset that has limited God and the displaying of His grandeur in your life. By resting in and experiencing the presence and glory of God, you will be empowered to receive and harness His truth, divine wisdom, revelation and supernatural faith to confidently realize, embrace and achieve your unique purpose and grand destiny in this new era!

God has given you a riveting new identity in this new era! Volume II inspires and imparts how to further unlock and mature your imagination to fulfill God's purposes for your life. Discover what it is and how to shed your worldly, carnal self—how to transition into your higher IAM state of being in Christ. Advance beyond the limitations of the third dimension, and gain supernatural knowledge of the mysterious workings of the unrestrictive, four-dimensional realm of the Spirit.

The marvelous design and divine workings of the inspired imagination is further unveiled in this third volume. You will gain applicable spiritual understanding of how to access, unlock and interpret the meanings of visions and dreams that God skillfully fashions within your imagination. You will discover how to access your God-given authority. You will unite with the Fire of God to believe, see and prophesy in the NOW realm of God's faith. Through a broadened understanding of God's Word and clear spiritual insights into the profound power of imaginative prayer, you will be able to access the answers to your prayers that have been waiting on you to discover from the Genesis of creation. *IMAGINE* Volume III will equip and fully transition you into your new and glory-purposed identity in Christ. Your faith in God will explode into the supernatural faith of God!

In this instructive and illuminating volume, you will gain divine knowledge about the healing power of the subconscious, God's imaginative power and creative miracles. Volume IV will challenge what you believe, see and reason as truth and will help you identify the hindrances to having your prayers answered. God is restoring His people as One New Man! By using your sanctified imagination, you will discover how to come into agreement with God in order to effectively release your prophetic voice in this new era. You will obtain valuable instruction on how to increase, advance and prosper for God's kingdom purposes.

This fifth volume of the *IMAGINE* series brings the concepts learned in previous volumes full circle. Now that you have believed, beheld and obtained your new identity, you will discover the keys to successfully maintain that identity. You will encounter God's creative power, divine desire, godly disciplines of the imagination and lasting growth. The time to advance is NOW! Volume V delivers sound biblical teachings of how to use your creative imagination to release and prophesy into your God-ordained destiny and the destinies of nations. You will acquire the necessary knowledge and wisdom to effectively operate, persevere and prosper as a true Son of God and as One New Man.

DecodeMyDream.com

ONLINE DREAM JOURNAL

Barbie Breathitt is excited that so many people in God's Kingdom are exploring the understanding of dreams. Barbie's 30 years of study and experience in biblically-based, spirit-led dream interpretation are available in an online learning experience.

DreamsDecoder.com and DecodeMyDream.com are our interactive web sites, impacting dreamers all over the world. We believe it is vitally important to record God-given dreams and to search out the messages they contain. The site provides a free online dream journal, dream evaluations, dream mapping, prophetic analysis and comprehensive dream certification training.

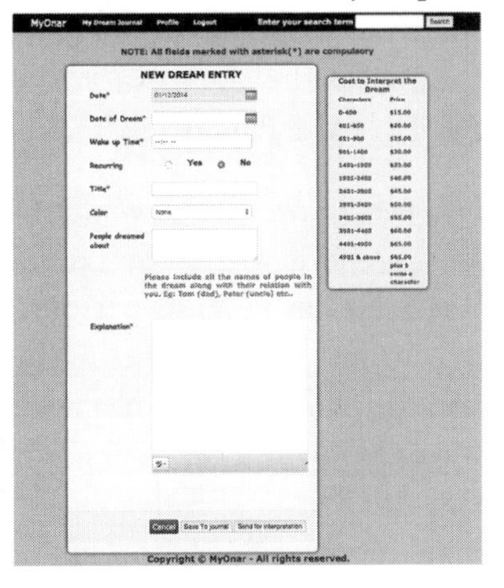

Sign up for your free online dream journal at DreamsDecoder.com. From the dream journal, you can easily submit your dreams for analysis by Barbie and our highly skilled dream analysts.

For additional resources by Dr. Barbie L. Breathitt, please visit
DreamsDecoder.com
Breath of the Spirit Ministries, Inc.
PO Box 1356 | Lake Dallas, TX 75065
(972) 253-6653

BOOKS

Dream Encounters–Seeing Your Destiny from God's Perspective is the "Rosetta Stone" to interpreting the illusive vapors of dreams. Uniquely inspired, and written to convince the greatest skeptics, and educate the most ardent believer, "Dream Encounters" will bring God's perspective, and understanding to the symbolic, visual, love letters, in the mysterious world of dreams. Take a journey into the sub–conscious night parables of the soul, to learn how dream truths impact your world; give direction, purpose, and destiny. Gain valuable keys to success by unlocking the mysteries of your dreams. Available as a paperback book, digital book or audio book.

Gateway to the Seer Realm: Look Again to See Beyond the Natural is written by Dr. Barbie Breathitt a gifted Seer who has years of personal experience interpreting dreams and ministering in the prophetic realm. You will gain valuable insights into understanding the ways of God and the divine supernatural realms of vision, dreams, angels, healing and destiny. Open new dimensions of revelation knowledge to learn how to access the Seer realm through intimate daily communication with God.

Dream Seer: Searching for the Face of the Invisible is written by Dr. Barbie L. Breathitt to help the reader understand the Seer Realms of angels, divine visions, the voice and presence of the Lord and dimensions where the ethereal vapors of our dreams will become substantial presences when we believe that anything is possible with God. God is the giver of dreams. Jesus is also the Redeemer. So, like a knight in shining armor, He comes to restore the dreams we have allowed to fall by the wayside. The Holy Spirit inspires us to recall the images He sent long ago. God has mapped out our future. He brings the events of the world to bear on our individual circumstances as He wills. When the events of our lives coincide with the correct timing of His plans, the next phase of our destiny ensues. The Holy Spirit knows the perfect time to bring the dreams and plans He has formulated to enable our purpose to come to pass.

There is only one right interpretation, God's. Every thing else is only shades of gray. Dream Interpreter will give you skill to correctly decipher the symbolism of your dreams. *Dream Interpreter* decodes symbols, types and shadows of images from a heavenly perspective in order to reveal the hidden mysteries that are contained within. Dream Interpreter will help the reader translate spiritual perceptions and happenings to accurately discern the events of the night. The gifted dream interpreter can decipher, convert and transform a concealed secret and then develop a blueprint for prosperity. You can learn to understand the evolution of vivid visions and dreams, the graphic picture language of nightmares and night terrors that come to visit and present truth about one's life. As a wise counsellor or life coach, dream interpreters fashion destiny bubbling up from the depths of the person's soul-potential to successfully guide the dreamer.

Acquiring a working knowledge of dream symbolism will enhance your ability to decipher the profound meanings of each symbol and then unlock the interpretation of every one of your dreams. Knowledge is power so learn to understand the mysteries that are hidden in your dreams. Their divine secrets will release your concealed potential so that you can design the destiny you have always longed for. Access the revelation knowledge stored in the pages of *A to Z Dream Symbology Dictionary*. Glean from ten thousand keywords and symbolic meanings that will inspire you to delve deeper into understanding why a certain animal, object, person, place, vehicle, article of clothing, tool, home, food, flower, weather pattern, action, emotion, color, or number appeared in your subconscious dream.

In her book, *Angels in God's Kingdom*, Dr. Barbie L. Breathitt propels readers beyond a natural understanding of the world around them to perceive and navigate the divine supernatural realms of the invisible world of angels. This one-of-a-kind comprehensive Biblical resource is full of progressive revelation and inspired spiritual truths. Dr. Barbie L. Breathitt covers fascinating topics detailing the origin, existence, and abode of angelic beings, their names, ministry functions, duties, and little known facts about the classifications of angels. She explores the nature of angels, the bold power of active faith and how the anointings of angels, seraphim, cherubim, heavenly creatures and host connect and guide us to and through the spirit world. Barbie shares her real life angelic encounters and the knowledge she has received through her diverse visitations, as well as her traumatic experience with the spirit of death. Discover the mystery of how recognizing the presence of powerful angels can redeem time when they are invited to step out of eternity to assist us in miracles, healing and deliverance. Learn how to prosper as the angels in God's Kingdom collide with the lawless evil forces of darkness and destruction. Gain spiritual understanding of how God's holy, intelligent angels clash with Satan's demons and diabolical fallen angels in today's modern world. Discover how the giants from the days of Noah are currently affecting society. And how we can defeat them through the blood of Jesus.

When Will My Dreams Come True? This handy booklet provides valuable detailed descriptions on dreams, visions and spiritual encounters. The information shared in these pages will educate the dreamer on the biblical techniques of dream interpretation. Through the study and application of the Hebrew alphabet and numbers, you will develop an Issachar anointing to discern the days, times and seasons of your dreams coming to pass. This collection of data research, priceless dream interpretation nuggets, gradient echelons of revelation, and prophetic vocabulary and terminology assembled in these pages will instruct dreamers on how to record and accurately interpret the meaning of their dreams, so they can pray, decree and declare them into being.

DREAM SYMBOL CARDS

These artistically designed dream symbol cards enable the dreamer to tap into the hidden meanings of the symbols that appear in many dreams and visions. These cards are also useful in helping the believer decipher the symbolic language that God uses to communicate through the revelatory realm of the Spirit. "God is speaking powerfully through dreams in this hour. So many believers are having significant dreams but do not always understand the significance of the symbols within them. Barbie Breathitt has done a marvellous job of preparing dream cards as a tremendous tool to help this process. They are very high quality and fully laminated for long-term use. I was impressed when I saw them." Patricia King XP Ministries (xpministries.com).

Acquire all of Barbie's artistically designed, laminated Dream Encounter Symbols Cards. They are available as single dream cards, in an excel spreadsheet or in spiral-bound collections.

Dream Encounters Symbols Volume I features the original 23 dream cards starter set with 1433 unique symbol definitions which makes an excellent gift for those who have a desire to learn the meanings of their dreams. The collection includes Animals, Apparel & Clothing, Body Parts, Color, Color and Music Healing, Creatures Great, Creatures Small, God's Dream Language, Going Places, Going More Places, Home Furnishings, Jewels, Musical Instruments, Numbers, People, Seers' Word of Knowledge Ministry Card, Spiritual, More Spiritual, Tools, U. S. State, Vehicles, and Weather and Natural Elements.

Dream Encounters Symbols Volume II has 18 different dream cards with 619 different symbol definitions. The collection includes Birds (4 dream symbol cards containing a myriad of positive and negative winged creatures), Bugs and Insects (3 cards), Money and Finance, Nutrition (5 cards outlining the meaning of different foods, sweets, meats and vegetables), Plants and Flowers (4 cards detail what different floral arrangements and bouquets represent. God is giving His Bride flowers in her dream. What is He saying to you?), and Varied contains a list of Frequent Dream Symbols.

Dream Encounters Symbols Volume III has an additional 29 spiral bound dream cards that combines 913 symbols complied in helpful categories for ease of study and use. The collection includes, Body Parts (an extensive compilation of 5 dream symbol cards), Building, Rooms & Structures (4 cards), People (12 individual cards listing careers, professions and callings), Spiritual & Military Weapons of War (4 dream symbol cards describing the spiritual weapons of prayer available to believers), and Vehicles (4 dream symbol cards boats, ships, trucks, cars, vans, airplanes, rockets and more).

Action Symbols Volume IV, has 13 artistically designed spiral bound dream symbol cards with 386 different movements such as flying, running, transporting, and translating actions.

Dream Sexology has 4 unique and informative dream symbol cards with 95 unique symbol definitions that explain the meanings of your intimate naked dream language.

Sports & Recreation Dream Symbols contains 13 dream symbol cards full of 321 different hobbies, sports, games and much more to help you take an active part in the game of life instead of sitting on the sidelines observing the excitement of others.

TEACHING SERIES

The Dream Encounter MP3 Downloads and Manual is designed to teach, train, activate, and impart the skills to interpret and understand how God communicates to us through dreams and visions of the night. Jesus continues to teach through night parables, in other words, inspired dreams. The Bible gives us three keys that will be used in the end-time revival and outpouring of the Holy Spirit. The course topics include: Dreams, Visions, Transportations, Translations, Lucid Dreams, Colors, Numbers, Dream Symbols, Dream Interpretation, and Dream Teams and Outreaches.

The Revelatory Encounter MP3 Downloads and Manual is a prophetic course designed to teach, train, activate, and impart the ability to hear God's voice for yourself and others. This training helps you recognize and remove hindrances to hearing God's still, small voice. The course topics include: Developing Godly Character and Integrity, Old and New Testament Prophets, False Prophets, Immature Prophets, God's Friends, Knowing God's Voice, Difference between the Gift of Prophecy and the Prophetic Office, Forms of Revelation, Four Categories of Prophecy, Spirit of Prophecy, Nine Gifts of the Holy Spirit, Interpretation, Application, The Seer, The Watchmen, Intercession, Prayer, Intimacy, Spiritual Authority, and Developing Prophetic Ministry Teams.

The Angelic Encounter MP3 downloads and Manual is a course that establishes a biblical foundation for the proof and ministry of angels. Topics include: What are Angels? Ministry of Angels; Types, Functions, and Characteristics of Angels; Satan and Fallen Angels; and Angels and the Death of the Saints. Barbie shares personal experiences of angelic visitations from her life.

The Healing Encounter MP3 Downloads and Manual is designed to teach, train, activate and impart the belief, skills and abilities to move in the healing ministry. Topics include: Introduction to Healing; Jesus, the Healer; Issues of the Heart; Four Aspects of Healing; The Faith Realm; Take Your Authority; You Get What You Expect; Miracles Today; Hindrances to Miracles; Suffering in Regards to Healing; God's Voice of Healing; You Must See it to Be it!; Keep Your Healing; Healing Scriptures; Baptism with the Holy Spirit; and Walking in the Healing Ministry.

OTHER RESOURCES

The Hand Prayer Points Chart is a reference card that matches illnesses and diseases with prayer points on the hand. Great for intercessors who need clear direction for their prayers.

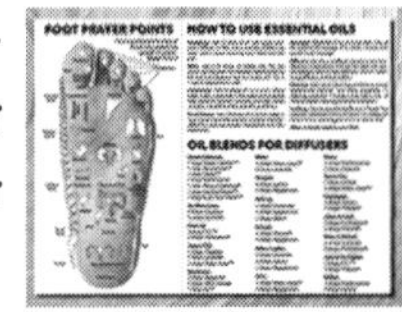

The Foot Prayer Points Chart is a reference card that matches the organs of the body, illnesses and diseases with prayer points on the foot. Great for intercessors who need clear direction for their prayers.

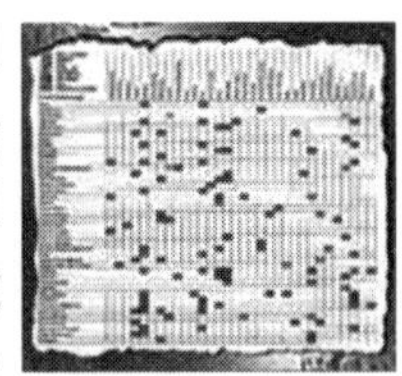

Healing Card is a reference card that matches illnesses and diseases with possible spiritual root causes. This Healing card is birthed from Barbie's ministry experiences and encounters of seasoned intercessors and those in healing ministries. Great for intercessors and individuals who need clear direction for their healing prayers.

Waking Words of Ancient Wisdom Make it a practice to notice the time on the digital clock as you awaken from a spiritually significant dream. The numbers displayed on the digital clock are often keys to help understand the message God is giving you in your dreams. Note the time on your clock, then look up the corresponding chapter and verse in the Bible. Allow the Holy Spirit to quicken the intended "Waking Words of Ancient Wisdom" to your heart and apply them in your life. This is a wonderful way to daily explore the Bible while you seek the deeper meanings of the treasures God is revealing to you through your dreams. Visit BarbieBreathitt.com to obtain detailed directions for use.

Dream Encounter Anointing Oil: Anoint yourself every night with this fragrant dream enhancing oil and pray for the Holy Spirit to visit you in your sleep. You will experience a heightened level of dreams, visions and visitations from the Spirit of God.

My Thoughts